# Technology in the Schools:
## Equity and Funding

John C. Arch, Editor

*Reference & Resource Series*





**Produced in cooperation with**
**NEA Instruction and Professional Development**

nea
PROFESSIONAL LIBRARY
National Education Association
Washington, D.C.

**Note**

The opinions expressed in this publication should not be construed as representing the policy or position of the National Education Association. Materials published as part of the Reference & Resource Series are intended to be discussion documents for teachers who are concerned with specialized interests of the profession.

**Library of Congress Cataloging-in-Publication Data**

Technology in the schools.

(Reference & resource series)
Bibliography: p.
1. Education—Data processing—Planning. 2. Educational technology—Finance. 3. Sex discrimination in education. I. Arch, John C. II. Series: Reference and resource series.
LB1028.43.T43 1986 371.3'07'8 86-18278
ISBN 0-8106-1535-5

# Technology in the Schools:
## Equity and Funding

John C. Arch, Editor

*Reference & Resource Series*

nea

# *Introduction: Equity and Funding*

**by John C. Arch**

*John C. Arch is Associate Professor of Mathematics and Computer Science, and Director of the Regional Computer Resource Center at Shippensburg University, Pennsylvania.*

## FUNDING

Many of the problems with funding computers in schools stem from the lack of clear-cut goals for educational computing. A question seldom asked is, what exactly are computers doing in schools anyway? Without a definite, clear answer to this question, adequate funding should not be forthcoming. With school budgets as tight as they are, educators should request money for computers only when there are sound educational reasons for doing so. Money should be spent on computers only if they can improve the quality of education.

The three generally accepted educational uses of computers are the following:

1. Computers used as tools; the best example is word processing. Other examples of tool programs are spreadsheets, data bases, and classroom and instructional magazines.
2. Computers as the object of study, or computer science. This is specifically mentioned in *A Nation at Risk* as one of the new basics in education required for today.
3. Use of computers to improve the delivery of instruction. The question of whether computers can be used to improve the quality of instruction in our schools has yet to be answered definitively. Software exists to deliver instruction in almost any subject area, but does the quality of the instruction improve? Research into this question has given us mixed results.

The dilemma for educators is to determine for which, if any, of these three uses funds should be expended. Expenditures for use 1, the use of computers as tools, are easy to justify. Word processors, spreadsheets, and the like, are widely used throughout our society. To be against them is like being against typewriters. No matter how loudly you object, no one is going to listen. The second use, the study of computer science, has the backing of a presidential commission (see *A Nation at Risk*). Expenditures for this use, too, are easily justified. Problems arise, however, with the third use, computers for instruction. Here educators cannot be so confident. Until better methodologies of instructional computing are developed, caution must be shown before spending money for this purpose.

Priorities may need to be reorganized, but the direction is obvious. At the present time, computers as tools and as objects of study are legitimate, defensible uses of computers in schools. Expenditures for these purposes should be looked upon as necessities.

Instructional computing, on the other hand, is experimental, in that it is not yet a proven means of delivering better instruction. More investigation into software development needs to be undertaken. Until then, schools that invest heavily in instructional computing are spending money on an unproved technology.

Alfred Bork in "Let's Test the Power of Interactive Technology" and David Moursund in "The Two Percent Solution—Funding for Use of Computers" present ideas whose time has arrived. Bork calls for a large-scale, six-year project to develop and test curriculum that utilizies the computer much more fully than existing curricula. But certainly the local districts cannot be expected to foot the bill for such a massive undertaking. Cake sales will not be enough. Before such a large-scale project gets underway, the federal government must commit to providing much, if not all, of the funding.

Moursund describes a practical plan for providing permanent, long-term funding for computers at the local level—all at a minimum of disruption to the rest of the budget.

## EQUITY

Why the big fuss over equity? Who cares that more boys than girls, more whites than minorities, more rich than poor, and more good math students than mathphobes have better access to computers? Answers to these questions can be found all around us. Computers are everywhere. People who lament the widespread use of computers can no more stop their spread than the Luddites could stop the development of the textile factories of nineteenth century England. All indications are that the use of computers will continue to expand at a rapid rate.

For better or worse, computers are *the* technology of our time and they will be for the foreseeable future. To limit the access of certain groups to computers is akin to limiting their access to reading and writing. Farfetched? Hardly. Computers are used not only in science and math, but also in libraries, law enforcement, space exploration, publishing, accounting, engineering, graphic art, film, and so on—the whole panoply of what we as humans do. More and more of our culture is being influenced, and in some cases dominated, by computers.

Are we as educators prepared to shut out women, minorities, the poor, and other groups from full participation, not only in the future but in the present as well? If not, then steps will have to be taken to assure equal access to all. If these groups are denied equal access, they will not be able to participate fully in the ongoing computerization of our society.

Unfortunately, many obstacles must be overcome, as is made clear by Percy Walcott in "Funding Computer Technology," Irene T. Miura and Robert D. Hess in "Enrollment Differences in Computer Camps and Summer Classes," and by Phyllis A. DuBois and Jane G. Schubert in "Do Your School Policies Provide Equal Access to Computers? Are You Sure?" Currently, computer clubs, camps, and courses are dominated by boys and the well-to-do. Many teachers have the mistaken belief that computers are appropriate only for certain types of students. A large number of schools establish meaningless math prerequisites for computer courses, which effectively eliminates many females from these courses. Inequities also exist among the different states and regions of the country.

Some solutions to one of the most perplexing of these problems, that of sex-based inequities, are offered by Jo Schuchat Sanders in ''Here's How You Can Help Girls Take Greater Advantage of School Computers.'' A controversial suggestion comes from Art Luehrmann in ''Programming for Boys, Word Processing for Girls.''

Eliminating these inequities will not be easy. It will necessitate long-term commitments of both time and money. But an equitable future requires such a commitment.

Finally, to round out the collection, you will find two contributions by Henry S. Kepner, Jr. ''The Information Age and the Schools'' presents an overview of the entire field of educational computing, while ''Suggested Readings for Computer Equity and Funding'' provides an annotated bibliography for those who are interested in learning more about either topic.

# *Let's Test the Power of Interactive Technology*

**by Alfred Bork**

*Alfred Bork is Professor of Education and Computer Science, Professor of Physics, and Director, Educational Technology Center, University of California-Irvine.*

The time has come to seriously evaluate the idea that interactive technology can significantly improve American education. Our nation's school system is dangerously weak, and few of the prescriptions offered for strengthening it are likely to be filled. We have enough evidence for the effectiveness of interactive technology to warrant a trial project, which, if successful, should lead to a major development effort.

## OUR EDUCATIONAL SYSTEM HAS SERIOUS PROBLEMS

The evidence for deficiencies in our educational system is so well known that I will not recite most of it here. I will refer only to problems of financing, to concerns about the quality of learning, and to circumstances of teachers.

*Financing.* During much of our history, the general population was happy to support public schools, but now education must fight for funds. Part of the reason is a growing resistance to taxes for any purpose (even though our taxes are low compared with other leading countries). We spend $140 billion each year on our schools. Because our present system is labor intensive, much of this is in salaries. Because of our national reluctance to put more money into education, teacher salaries are low: recent data from the National Education Association put the average salary at $23,000, the lowest average salary in the United States for a position requiring a university degree. To summarize, our schools are not well funded, and the prospects for better funding are poor.

*Learning Outcomes.* It is not easy to measure quality of learning, but most studies about education in the United States have concluded that the quality is relatively poor and probably declining. From the standpoint of international economic competition, it is disturbing to note that international testing shows our students lag behind those in competing countries. From a different point of view, Gallup polls show that about half the parents in the United States are unhappy with the schools their children attend. Further, many courses are old and do not reflect current knowledge and attitudes.

*Teachers.* A third factor is the condition of the teaching profession. As already noted, teacher salaries are low. The working conditions for teachers are also poor

From *Educational Leadership* (March 1986): 36–37. Reprinted with permission of the Association for Supervision and Curriculum Development. 

compared with many other occupations. Hence it is not surprising that fewer able university students are now considering teaching as a career. Schools of education have had drastic declines in the number of students preparing for teaching and in the quality of students entering their programs. We train, for example, about one fifth of the number of mathematics teachers now that we did ten years ago!

Over half of the schools in the United States, mostly those in rural areas, no longer teach advanced science and mathematics courses, because they no longer have qualified teachers in these areas. The National Science Teachers Association estimates that 30 percent of the existing science teachers are highly inadequate. Many of our existing teachers will retire in the next decade, and we have at present little prospect of replacing them with excellent new teachers.

Most of the solutions being suggested for these problems are inadequate. We must find new answers.

## A POWERFUL NEW LEARNING TECHNOLOGY IS AVAILABLE

Not since the printing press has a technology had such far-reaching ramifications for education. The most important advantage of the computer is that it allows learning to be interactive for all students. In earlier eras most learning was interactive, with the student playing an active role in the process. Even today a few can afford private tutors or other highly interactive approaches. But with the need for more and more people to be educated—both because of population increases and because education has come to be considered a human right—we have moved to less interactive learning approaches: the lecture and the textbook.

At least two types of interaction characterize good computer learning situations: interaction between students and the computer, and interaction among students themselves. Consider two or three students working together, using a highly interactive computer program. The learning sequence proceeds Socratic fashion as the computer asks questions, perhaps every 15 or 20 seconds. The questions are in ordinary everyday language, and the answers are free form, with students typing in anything they wish. Student answers receive reasonable replies, and lead to new questions. (We already have working examples of such Socratic dialogues available on computers.) One type of interaction, then, is between the student and the computer.

But the computer also stimulates another type of interaction: discussion among the students as they work together at the computer. There is more peer interaction in this kind of setting than there is in most current classrooms—and it is focused on the learning process. Students help each other to understand the material, a powerful learning aid.

One very important aspect of interactive technology is that the learning activity can be specifically suited to each individual. Because the student is frequently responding, the computer can build up information about the strengths and weaknesses of that particular student. This allows learning to be individualized, so that every student can receive an individually tailored learning sequence. Another aspect of the computer's flexibility is that students can take as much or as little time as necessary at each step in the learning process. Because they receive only the help they need, most students learn more efficiently.

Unfortunately, most computer-based materials do not make appropriate use of even existing capabilities, let alone those currently being developed. Much of the available software is primitive. Because educators have not seen materials with the characteristics I have described, they tend to judge the computer on the basis of the limited modules they have seen. For this reason and others, many people are not convinced that computer-based learning modules could be the basis for a new educational system. Education has continued so long in its present mold that many think of the present system as eternal.

What is more, even computer enthusiasts will freely admit that a fully developed computer-based educational system is far, far away from our current limited use of computers. We need to scale up by many orders of magnitude to make a major difference, and doing so is risky because we have little experience in developing and using such materials.

## AN EMPIRICAL APPROACH

The potential value of such an effort need not be debated on a philosophical level, however; we can use an empirical approach. I propose a six-year trial project, the first years of which would be devoted primarily to development of curriculum meaterials, with a gradual shift to implementation and evaluation.

In the trial project, about 20 full-scale courses should be developed covering the educational spectrum in age and subject areas. To encourage a wide variety of approaches, different agencies would be involved, with no agency developing more than two courses. We should not expect all the new courses to be successful, but I believe we would find that some would be highly competitive with conventional instruction.

If the experiment is successful, we should then proceed to develop new technology-based courses in all subject areas. In the process we would expect to learn more about how to design such computer-based curricula, but should continue to insist upon a diversity of approaches; there should never be a single official philosophy governing course development or structure.

Another type of diversity is also important. Our educational system, unlike those of some other countries, is not planned at the national level. In principle at least, local schools can make independent choices (although in practice these choices are often affected by the limited availability of learning materials). Because we cherish this diversity, it will not be sufficient to have only a single course in a given area. For example, there should be not one but several beginning high school algebra courses. All courses should be designed to be as flexible as possible, so that a skilled teacher would be able to adapt the materials to the local situation and perhaps even combine components from several sources.

A critical issue in this connection is the effect on teachers. Technology gives us the possibility of an educational system requiring fewer teachers, but this should not be perceived as a threat to the teaching profession, because it also makes possible new and more interesting roles for well-qualified teachers.

The proposed full-scale development would be an extensive activity, but not unrealistic compared to other projects we have undertaken as a country, such as putting a man on the moon. It is not unlike some large-scale efforts in science, such as the building of huge accelerators, or similar efforts in industry. Our nation has considerable expertise in the management of such projects. The full developmental activity would occupy a period of about eight years. I estimate the cost to be about one billion dollars a year, or about ten billion dollars altogether.

Accompanying the development would be evaluation, both formative and summative. After the major development period there would be continuing development of new courses, but at a reduced scale. Summative evaluations, advances in knowledge, and new approaches to learning would be factors to consider in deciding where continuing development was necessary.

Developing the new curriculum would, of course, be only part of the process. At least as difficult would be installing the system in schools, including teacher training. Those responsible would need to be fully aware of the research on school cultures and on processes for bringing about extensive changes in large social systems.

## WE SHOULD TRY

I have suggested in this brief [chapter] a process that could lead to far better learning for many students. Details are missing; leadership would be needed to carry it out; but such a process could give us, once again, the best educational system in the world. The technology exists, and the cost, compared to other national efforts, is reasonable. We need not argue about how successful such an effort would be; we should try it, in a carefully controlled experiment, and find out.

# *The Two Percent Solution—Funding for Use of Computers*

**by David Moursund**

*David Moursund is the president of the International Council for Computers in Education and editor of* The Computing Teacher.

How much money schools should be spending for instructional use of computers depends upon the goals set by the school or district.

But that answer is less than satisfying to administrators in a school district just beginning to make a serious commitment to the instructional use of computers. Administrators need help in determining the level of expenses and nature of the commitment that may be necessary over the long run.

## ANALYSIS HELPS UNDERSTANDING

The Two Percent Solution is a simple idea. Let's see what could happen if a school district budgeted two percent of its funds, year after year, for instructional computing. Some districts might obtain this level of funding by a reallocation of current funds. But since budgets have been so tight for so long, this is unlikely in most districts. As an alternative, one could imagine the taxpayers in a district passing a special perpetual tax that adds two percent to the district's budget. Or, one might imagine a one percent tax and a reallocation of current funds to generate the other one percent. An analysis of how two percent of a district's current budget might be used for instructional computing helps one to understand how much money is actually needed.

## WHY TWO PERCENT?

Two percent is an arbitrary figure, but one can find many colleges and universities that have that level of expenditure for instructional computing purposes. Also, the use of a percentage figure relates expenditures to a district's overall funding level. This is important because funding levels vary widely. A recent issue of *The Wall Street Journal* discussed a school in Alaska that had a budget of $16,000 per student per year. The same article noted that the average for the United States is about $2,500 per student per year, with some states having an average per-pupil yearly expenditure of under $2,000.

Where will the two percent go? I suggest four major categories of expenditures, with a reasonable level of funding for each. A fifth category, a contingency fund, is

Reprinted with permission from *The Computing Teacher*, March 1984, vol. 11, no. 7. Published by the International Council for Computers in Education.

suggested to take care of unforeseen expenses. Keep in mind that these are merely suggestions; they can lead to insight into what a particular school district might do.

1. **Hardware:** Approximately one-half of the total funds.
2. **Software, print materials and other support materials:** Approximately one-sixth of the total funds.
3. **Inservice education:** Approximately one-twelfth of the total funds. This provides initial and continuing training for administrators, teachers, support personnel and aides.
4. **Computer coordinators:** Approximately one-sixth of the total funds. This might be used at both a district and a building level.
5. **Contingency:** Approximately one-twelfth of the total funds. In the first year, all of this might be used to supplement inservice education. In subsequent years it might be used in the other categories, or for some new purpose such as remodeling a room for a computer lab.

This sort of allocation assumes that office space, janitorial services, ongoing administrative and staff support, and other miscellaneous expenses will be part of the general school district budget and will not be specifically deducted from instructional computing funds.

To make this concrete, suppose we look at a school district with 5,000 students and a budget of $2,500 per student per year. The Two Percent Solution allocates $50 per student per year for instructional computing.

| Category | Per Pupil | Total |
|---|---|---|
| 1. Hardware | $25.00 | $125,000 |
| 2. Software & Materials | $ 8.33 | $ 41,667 |
| 3. Inservice Education | $ 4.17 | $ 20,833 |
| 4. Coordinators | $ 8.33 | $ 41,667 |
| 5. Contingency | $ 4.17 | $ 20,833 |

## WHAT CAN WE BUY?

The figure that tends to be most interesting to school district administrators is the money for hardware. What can one buy with $25 per student per year? The answer obviously depends upon the particular equipment being purchased. A recent ad in my town's local newspaper indicated one could purchase a 64K machine with one disk drive, printer and monochrome monitor for about $900. The ad was for a very widely sold computer system from a reputable local dealer.

The same newspaper contained an ad for a Timex-Sinclair Model 1000 system, 16K expansion module and three software tapes at a special discount price of $29.97. A tape recorder and television set are needed to make this into a usable system.

The $900 figure might be considered adequate for a low to middle-price microcomputer. You can expect that the quality of machine that this amount of money can buy will continue to improve rapidly in the future. Many school districts are purchasing more expensive microcomputers, but they usually obtain a substantial discount from the list price.

Now a couple of assumptions are needed. A typical school doesn't want a printer on every microcomputer, and it's likely the school will want some dual disk systems. As a school obtains a quantity of machines, it is likely some will be networked using a floppy or hard disk system. This may cut the average cost of a user station. Let us assume that the average cost of a user station will be about $900. Let's also assume that such systems will have a four-year life span, with maintenance costs averaging $100 per machine over the four years. An equivalent way of expressing this is to assume that $1,000 provides a user station that functions for four years and is then completely worn out.

A particular school district may decide to purchase computers costing much more than is assumed above. Such machines might have a longer life span, different maintenance costs and so on. The point is, the explicit example given here serves as a model a district can use to analyze its own situation.

Continuing the example, the first year's funds would purchase approximately one machine per 40 students. (The current average in the United States is approximately one machine per 120 students, or a third of what would be achieved in the first year.) The second year's funds would bring the average to one machine per 20 students; the steady state situation in the fourth and subsequent years would be one machine per 10 students. This analysis ignores whatever computers a district might already own.

An average of one machine per 10 students is equivalent to about a half-hour of machine time per student per day. If computers are going to have a significant impact upon our overall educational system, we should be able to see the beginning of the impact with this average level of computer usage.

This hardware analysis suggests that an average school district, by spending one percent of its budget every year for hardware, will eventually have about one microcomputer per 10 students. That is about 12 times the current average in the United States. If computer prices continue to decline, or if machines have a longer life span, then an even higher ratio will be achieved. Alternately, if a district selects more expensive hardware, it will achieve a lower ratio of machines per student.

The money allocated for software, manuals, books, films and related support material is substantial but may prove inadequate, as classroom sets of textbooks and expendable workbooks may be quite expensive. One way to analyze this is to look at various categories of instructional computing. The categories I use are learning/teaching about computers, learning/teaching using computers and learning/teaching incorporating computers. Each category requires differing amounts and types of software, support materials and teacher knowledge.

Learning/teaching about computers requires relatively little software beyond the language translators and operating system. It does require books, films and other media, and it requires quite knowledgeable teachers.

Learning/teaching using computers (usually called computer-assisted learning) can require a substantial software library. Currently the costs of such software are high and the total quantity of good software is still quite limited. We can expect a continued rapid growth in the availability of good computer-assisted learning software. We will probably find that vendors will make available multiple copies of software, or software for local networks, at quite good prices.

Learning/teaching incorporating computers requires changes in the content of the conventional curriculum. A typing course might become a word processing course, requiring word processing software and perhaps a typing tutor program. A bookkeeping course might be substantially changed by providing electronic spreadsheet and accounting software. A science lab might be changed by a package of programs for the on-line control of experiments and the collection and processing of data. A math course might require a substantial library of graphic, equation-solving and symbol-manipulation software.

A different way to view this expenditure category is that the $1,000 machine will have $333 of software, print materials and other support materials. This is quite a bit if all of these materials have a long lifespan and can be used by a variety of students. For example, a single rental film might be viewed by many hundreds of students and a reference book may be useful for several years. A growing library of commerical software might be supplemented by carefully screened public domain software.

The money for inservice education of administrators, teachers, support personnel and aides will allow for initial and continued growth in their knowledge and skills. If a district has not yet put much money into computer-related inservice education, the first year's expenditures probably need to be above one-twelfth of the total funds. This can be done by drawing upon the contingency fund.

It is important to realize that inservice education must continue beyond the initial effort. The level of knowledge needed when there is only one microcomputer per 120 students is quite different from what is needed when there is one microcomputer for every 10 students. At this level we could begin to see substantial changes in the content of current non-computer courses. This will require extensive inservice education as well as funds to support curriculum development and revision.

The funds and training effort need not be evenly spread among all educators. Likely it will prove desirable for each school to have a building-level coordinator with some release time from regular teaching duties. While all educators need an elementary working-tool level of computer knowledge, these building-level coordinators will need substantially more knowledge as part of their jobs. They will pass on some of their knowledge and skill. Some of the inservice education funds could be used to facilitate this much higher level of training.

Finally, we come to the computer coordinator funds. In four years a 5,000-student school district will have about 500 microcomputer systems valued at approximately a half-million dollars. The district may have several hundred thousand dollars invested in software and other support materials. This is a substantial investment. A district computer coordinator will have a wide range of duties including supervising hardware and software acquisition, assisting in a large inservice education program, and working with curriculum committees to integrate computers into the curriculum.

Some of the district computer coordinator funds might be used at the building level—especially in large districts. The idea of building-level computer coordinators is very important. Consider an elementary school with 400-500 students. Under the model being discussed, this school might eventually have 40 or more microcomputers.

The fifth category, the contingency fund, can be used for a wide variety of purposes. As stated earlier, it might be used to supplement teacher inservice monies, especially in the beginning, or for remodeling.

Funds could also be provided for:

- Accessing large-scale data banks;
- Special-purpose peripherals such as videodisc equipment;
- Hardware and software for students to borrow for home use;
- Establishing a community (neighborhood) school to provide community access to instructional computing equipment.

Possible uses of the contingency fund seem endless.

## CONCLUSION

The Two Percent Solution provides an interesting model to explore certain aspects of the future of computers in instruction. Most important is the idea of a permanent commitment to a reasonable level of funding. Most school districts have not yet made this sort of commitment. They are purchasing equipment using entitlement funds, block grants, grants from foundations, money from parent-teacher organizations, and so on. They are giving "one-shot" teacher training workshops with little or no follow-up or opportunity for deeper training. They have not yet done the necessary planning for computers to have a significant and continuing long-term impact upon the overall content and process of education.

Two percent is a good initial goal. It is enough money to establish a solid program of instructional use of computers. Two percent will probably prove quite inadequate over the long run. Perhaps a few years from now I will be writing an editorial on The Five Percent Solution.

# *Funding Computer Technology*

**by Percy Walcott**

*Percy Walcott is a Research Specialist with NEA Research.*

The nation is facing a rapid expansion of computers in the classroom. In the Fall of 1984 there were more than half a million; by the end of the 1984-85 school year, acquisitions will make the figure go to over one million; and by the end of this decade, three million computers will be used in the public schools.

Software sales to schools totaled $22 million back in 1982, and sales of $300 million are expected by 1987.

How are the schools paying for their new high technology tool?

In the beginning, a computer buff, usually a math or science teacher, would talk the principal into buying the school a computer. Now everyone, school boards, administrators, teachers, parents, and of course, computer vendors, are encouraging schools to buy computers.

The funds come from numerous sources including the U.S. Department of Education through federal block grants administered by state and local governments; state and local government school budgets; Parent-Teacher Association fundraisers; and some private corporations.

A survey of ten large school districts done by Electronic Learning revealed:

- Federal funds are very limited.
- Individual school projects and PTA fundraisers add substantial revenues.
- School officials plan to solicit funds from private corporations also in the future.

Houston Independent School District used the following funding strategy. It spent $2.2 million on hardware, software, electrical work, and computer-related curriculum materials with state, local, and federal sources, each accounting for one-third. Of the federal funds, mostly Chapter 1 funds were used. The local one-third share came through PTA participation in a matching fund where the district matched whatever a school raised for equipment purchases.

In Philadelphia, funds to purchase computers came from Home and School association gifts, the schools' own budgets, mini-grants from state funds, and a few federal dollars. The superintendent said he intended to seek out corporate gifts. The district has a five-year plan underway to put a 34-station lab per 1000 students in each secondary school and to put an 18-station lab in each elementary school.

At the federal agency level, Congress has appropriated $9.9 million for FY 1985 to fund the Education for Economic Security Act, P.L. 98-377, Title 11. This law was enacted to meet the needs identified in "A Nation at Risk" and other reports on the condition of education. The funds, distributed as discretionary grants from the Secretary of Education, are to assist projects of national significance in math, science, computer technology, and foreign languages.

---

Reprinted from *Collective Bargaining Quarterly*, vol. 8, no. 3, December 1985.

Under Title VI of the same P.L. 98-377, an Excellence in Education Program has been funded to the tune of $5 million for FY 1985. Its intent is to give grant assistance to local education agencies which are conducting projects of excellence in individual public schools. Special school awards (more money) will go to schools which obtain financial contributions from the private sector to support their excellence projects.

In the scheme of things, these two federal programs cannot supply the nation's schools with computers, so schools will continue to look to state and local government sources and to PTA fundraisers and to private sources for funds.

## IMPLICATIONS FOR EQUITY

The infusion of computer technology into schools introduces a new set of equity questions involving such concerns as: Are the differences in acquiring computer hardware in school systems across the nation occurring in a manner resulting in inequities? What software will different users get? Will richer suburban school populations afford more sophisticated software thereby promoting higher-order learning skills? Will the drill and practice software be mostly consumed by schools on the lower end of the socio-economic pole? And will this drill and practice software be more commonly called up for females, Blacks and other minorities, and students with limited English proficiency?

Panelists at the first World Conference on Computers in Education raised similar concerns about equity.

One panelist expressed fear that the increased private ownership of information services which is being spurred by the high-technology industry could limit freedom of information to only members of the privileged class. Children who have computers at home and use them as a normal, everyday tool of life have a "significant" advantage over those who work on computers for an hour a week at school, the panelist believed.

Another panelist noted that minority children are less likely to use computers at school and at home than their wealthier white counterparts. The average annual income of families with home computers is $35,000 to $40,000. Meanwhile, the median income for Black families is below $25,000 and below $12,000 for single Black female heads of households. These families are unlikely to own a home computer.

Considering the relative availability of computers in the schools which ethnic minorities attend, they suffer a comparative disadvantage there as well. Southern and Western states have the highest concentration of Black and Hispanic Americans, and these states have the lowest computer-to-student ratios in the country, the panelist noted.

More research is needed before one can make a determination that inequities in the availability of computers to certain school children exist to such an extent that the inequities must be remedied.

One important consideration is what happens between the computer haves and the computer have-nots? One study referred to by Henry Levin shows cross-age tutoring yielding two times better gains in achievement than computer-assisted instruction; but many more studies must be done before we can know for certain.

Another consideration is that computers at home are used principally for entertainment; therefore children who have computers at home might have a "significant" advantage over less privileged children in computer games, not necessarily in academic achievement.

Further, the information, drills and procedures that might be called up on the screen of a computer can certainly be replicated on the pages of a book. While the computer is a useful modern tool, failure to be exposed to a computer might not be *ipso facto* a deprivation of a thorough and efficient education in school.

The explosion and imminent proliferation of computers in classrooms might well be the result of our cultural tendency to keep up with the Joneses, aided and abetted by an aggressive computer sales force.

As an aspect of this explosion, we need to know how much time the computer is being used and how much time it is idle, so efficient scheduling becomes possible and funds can be put to their best use. We must find out more about how the computer enhances the human mind (if it does) and how it helps in the learning process before we can ask responsible parties to ensure the equitable availability of computers to all students.

The statistical information we have gathered on the availability of computers in schools does show the southeast region lagging behind the rest of the nation. The national average number of 75 students per computer is well exceeded by North and South Carolina, Tennessee, Alabama, Georgia, Louisiana, and Mississippi, which means students in these states have fewer computers to use compared with students elsewhere in the nation. However, by this writing the number of computers in schools would have doubled, reaching more than a million computers in our nation's schools. Whether states in the southeast region will account for a large proportion of the increase and make up the gap in computers for students, we do not know. The acquisition of computers in schools is in its growth phase we do not know when it will stop. We have no basis to ascertain what number of students per computer is the right or reasonable quantity, so we cannot define equity at this time. What the research shows so far is that schools and communities are doing their best to put a reasonable number of computers into their schools.

## WHAT WILL THE FUTURE BRING?

To predict what the future holds we must have a firm grasp of present realities. Currently, the computer is used five different ways in schools:

1. For computer-assisted instruction where the student interacts with the computer engaging in drill and practice, tutorials, simulations, and problem solving.

2. For computer-managed instruction where the computer serves as a support tool for the teacher and principal in diagnosing learning difficulties; prescribing appropriate learning materials and activities; monitoring student progress; generating test scores; managing the curriculum; and providing reports on students.

3. For education administrative applications: attendance records, test scoring, data analysis and reporting, or maintaining individualized education plans.

4. For tool applications and instruction, including word processing and graphs.

5. As an object of instruction for introductory courses in computers, and for programming.

In the early 1980's nearly all the commercially available software was used for computer-assisted instruction in a drill and practice mode, but now 75 percent of software use in schools is for drill and practice. As for the other four uses—

- Computer-managed instruction represents between 10 to 20 percent of current computer use in schools.
- Administrative uses of computers have only recently begun to emerge as software becomes available and school data processing units accept the more modern microcomputers.
- Meanwhile, computer use in tool applications increased dramatically in 1984; these are mainly word processing packages used for composing stories, and computer graphics for drawing and creating beyond the limitations of letters in the alphabet, or beyond the limitations of the nine real numbers we use for counting.
- The final use listed occurs at the elementary level and in high school introductory courses, In this use, most teachers indicate their purpose for having a computer in the classroom is to teach students how to use a computer, as much as it is to discuss how computers are being used in our lives.

## Hands-on Application

The amount of time students spend actually using the computer is an important consideration. Studies show computers are used for relatively short periods of time during the instructional week. The typical elementary student spends only about 20 minutes per week on a computer, and the typical secondary student spends about 45 minutes per week on the computer. An optimum amount of time must be spent on any learning task to produce a positive effect on skills and knowledge being mastered. Some experts believe using the computer 20 minutes per week is too brief to make any difference in learning outcomes.

## Policy Makers

State governments meanwhile are increasingly encouraging the use of computers in schools. Before 1981, only seven states had state-wide policies on education technology. Since then, 40 more states have developed policies or initiatives to encourage using computers in schools.

## Software

The expectations people are developing regarding the improvements computers can cause in school may be realized only when the delivery of software is properly managed and controlled.

It will take quality software to help improve student performance. Such software must—

- allow for easy operation;
- be accompanied by clear documentation;
- provide opportunities for students to control the learning process;

- provide interaction, feedback, and reward;
- allow students and teachers to set goals and evaluate themselves;
- use the full range of hardware capabilities such as graphs, sound, and color;
- include the important concepts and related facts of a subject matter;
- be easily integrated into the curriculum; and
- include student record-keeping capabilities, and be able to monitor student progress.

## Implementing and Organizing

Successfully integrating the computer into the classroom can be achieved only by systematic planning.

Courseware selection must involve teachers and teachers must be trained to use the specific courseware and applications prior to actual use in the classroom; also, students should be afforded self-pacing for the best results in achievement.

## What the Future Holds

Software distributed by electronic means is expected to replace current purchases of courseware packages; this could increase networking, cut costs, and ultimately make computer learning more widely available across all school systems.

The National Information Utilities Corporation describes the concept as follows:

> Courseware is entered into a central system and is transmitted through an uplink to a satellite. The satellite sends it to a local transmitter and the courseware is then broadcast directly to a host computer in a district school.
>
> This digitized data can be transmitted 30 times faster than current networks which use telephone lines.
>
> Students in the classroom would use computers which access the courseware under the teacher's control. The school would pay a user fee based on the type and amount of courseware used.

Meanwhile, the home computer market is expanding. Computer-assisted instruction in schools will dovetail with increased computer home use, and by the end of this decade, software available in schools will be available at home too.

Approaching the end of this decade, teachers will come to view CAI drill and practice as a way to reduce repetitious teaching tasks. They will view it as a helpful distraction for disruptive students, and as a patient, nonjudgmental friend for slower learners in the classroom.

Both teachers and administrators will regard the computer as a job aid which helps them manage individualized instruction and reduces the time they spend doing paper work.

The teaching profession can be affected in one of three ways by the infusion of computers in the classroom.

First, if teachers determine the suitability of software and manage its use, their image might be enhanced. Comparisons between teaching and professions in industry could be made easier when the two share similar job factors such as managing and manipulating high technology. Teachers' just claims for higher pay could be made more clear as the public sees some similarities between teachers' tasks and those of high-paid professionals in industry.

Second, if administrators decide the suitability of software and determine its classroom use, teacher responsibilities might be decreased. A "deskilling" of the profession could follow, as more instructional activity is turned over to the computer and as the computer tests and measures student skills.

Third, neither of these two scenarios might ensue, and the computer might quietly take its place in the classroom.

The following pages contain recent data on student microcomputer use by state and school district (reprinted by courtesy of Quality Education Data, Inc., Denver, Colorado).

## REFERENCES


1. Anderson, Ronald E., and others, "Computer Inequities in Opportunities for Computer Literacy." Minnesota University, Minneapolis. Minnesota Research and Evaluation Center, September, 1983.
2. *Educational Research*, Vol. 14, No. 5, May, 1985.
3. Educational Turnkey Systems, Inc., "Uses of Computers in Education." National Commission for Employment Policy, Report No. RR-85-07, Washington, D.C. April 1985.
4. *Electronic Learning*, Vol. 3, No. 6, March, 1984.
5. Federal Register, Vol. 49, No. 230, pp. 46755, 46761.
6. Gold, Deborah L., "Inequitable Computer Use in Schools Said to Endanger Freedom of Information." *Education Daily*, pp. 4, 5; August 6, 1985.
7. Hamilton, Patricia, and Casserly, Michael D., "Survey and Analysis of Technology in the Great Cities." Council of Great City Schools, Washington, D.C. November, 1983.
8. Levin, Henry M., "Costs and Cost-Effectiveness of Computer-Assisted Instruction." IFG Project Report No. 84-A21, Stanford University, September, 1984.
9. Lipkin, John, "Equity and Microcomputer Use in American Public Education." ECS Working Paper LEC 83-15. Education Commission of the States, Denver, Colorado. Law and Education Center, September, 1983.
10. Quality Education Data, Inc., "Microcomputer Usage in Schools 1984–1985." Denver, Colorado. March, 1985.
11. Reisner, Elizabeth R., "The Use of Computers in Instruction Supported Under Chapter I of the Education and Improvement Act." Policy Studies Assoc., Inc. Washington, D.C. September, 1983.
12. *School Uses of Microcomputers: Reports from a National Survey*. Issue No. 3, October, 1983; Issue No. 4, February, 1984. Johns Hopkins University, Baltimore, MD. Center for Social Organization of Schools.

## NUMBER OF STUDENTS PER MICRO BY STATE

| Rank 85 | State | Rank 84 | Rank 83 | No. of Students | No. of Units | Students per Micro |
|---|---|---|---|---|---|---|
| 1 | Alaska | 1 | 12 | 99,711 | 5,779 | 17.25 |
| 2 | Rhode Island | 18 | 38 | 136,336 | 6,428 | 21.21 |
| 3 | Minnesota | 2 | 2 | 726,230 | 24,552 | 29.58 |
| 4 | Wyoming | 4 | 7 | 100,945 | 3,370 | 29.96 |
| 5 | South Dakota | 3 | 1 | 122,901 | 3,604 | 34.10 |
| 6 | Colorado | 5 | 9 | 544,072 | 15,666 | 34.72 |
| 7 | Oregon | 7 | 19 | 442,303 | 12,479 | 35.44 |
| 8 | New Mexico | 21 | 30 | 260,980 | 7,293 | 35.79 |
| 9 | Washington | 11 | 10 | 728,817 | 18,934 | 38.49 |
| 10 | Connecticut | 8 | 25 | 465,359 | 11,845 | 39.29 |
| 11 | Nebraska | 9 | 11 | 264,806 | 6,598 | 40.13 |
| 12 | Indiana | 12 | 18 | 975,918 | 24,251 | 40.24 |
| 13 | Dist. of Col. | 48 | 24 | 87,927 | 2,131 | 41.26 |
| 14 | Florida | 20 | 14 | 1,528,504 | 36,281 | 42.13 |
| 15 | Kansas | 14 | 6 | 404,658 | 9,343 | 43.31 |
| 16 | West Virginia | 22 | 41 | 371,845 | 8,562 | 43.43 |
| 17 | Massachusetts | 30 | 13 | 874,486 | 19,686 | 44.42 |
| 18 | Montana | 6 | 3 | 161,715 | 3,633 | 44.51 |
| 19 | Arizona | 13 | 21 | 527,332 | 11,752 | 44.87 |
| 20 | North Dakota | 10 | 22 | 118,627 | 2,614 | 45.38 |
| 21 | Iowa | 17 | 5 | 494,715 | 10,833 | 45.67 |
| 22 | Utah | 23 | 8 | 388,357 | 8,133 | 47.75 |
| 23 | Vermont | 16 | 4 | 92,006 | 1,923 | 47.85 |
| 24 | Nevada | 19 | 35 | 151,599 | 3,167 | 47.87 |
| 25 | Wisconsin | 15 | 15 | 804,216 | 16,539 | 48.63 |
| 26 | New York | 36 | 26 | 2,653,839 | 44,067 | 49.08 |
| 27 | Texas | 33 | 33 | 3,026,529 | 60,234 | 50.25 |
| 28 | Michigan | 25 | 17 | 1,633,432 | 32,242 | 50.66 |
| 29 | New Jersey | 28 | 20 | 1,155,470 | 22,759 | 50.77 |
| 30 | Oklahoma | 26 | 16 | 619,248 | 12,133 | 51.04 |
| 31 | Illinois | 41 | 27 | 1,834,680 | 33,613 | 54.58 |
| 32 | Idaho | 35 | 29 | 206,777 | 3,775 | 54.78 |
| 33 | North Carolina | 43 | 45 | 1,099,278 | 19,959 | 55.08 |
| 34 | Pennsylvania | 31 | 36 | 1,695,741 | 30,366 | 55.84 |
| 35 | Maryland | 34 | 43 | 670,647 | 11,945 | 56.14 |
| 36 | Maine | 29 | 28 | 208,525 | 3,708 | 56.24 |
| 37 | South Carolina | 47 | 46 | 613,134 | 10,705 | 57.28 |
| 38 | Virginia | 39 | 37 | 977,923 | 16,916 | 57.81 |
| 39 | Tennessee | 45 | 44 | 826,291 | 14,206 | 58.16 |
| 40 | Kentucky | 32 | 42 | 672,139 | 11,545 | 58.22 |
| 41 | Delaware | 24 | 31 | 95,459 | 1,600 | 59.66 |
| 42 | Arkansas | 27 | 34 | 436,489 | 7,275 | 60.00 |
| 43 | California | 44 | 32 | 4,331,876 | 70,888 | 61.11 |
| 44 | Ohio | 40 | 40 | 1,850,747 | 29,592 | 62.54 |
| 45 | Missouri | 37 | 39 | 809,696 | 12,889 | 62.82 |
| 46 | Alabama | 46 | 49 | 724,512 | 11,241 | 64.45 |
| 47 | New Hampshire | 42 | 23 | 156,026 | 2,346 | 66.51 |
| 48 | Georgia | 49 | 47 | 1,151,359 | 15,321 | 75.15 |
| 49 | Mississippi | 51 | 50 | 464,864 | 6,052 | 76.81 |
| 50 | Louisiana | 50 | 48 | 781,346 | 9,343 | 83.63 |
| 51 | Hawaii | 38 | 51 | 171,000 | 1,984 | 86.19 |
| TOTAL | | | | 39,741,392 | 772,088 | 51.47 |

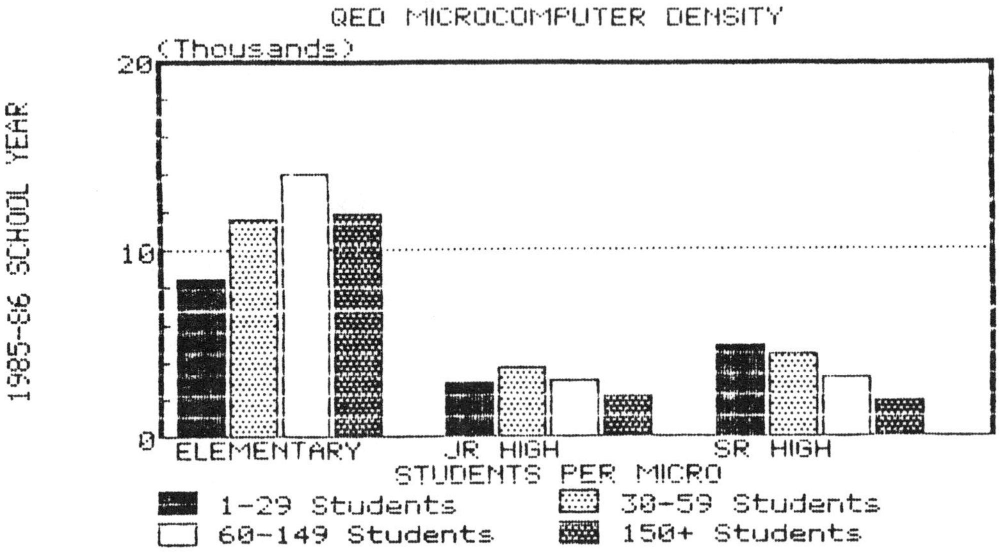


Note that even elementary schools have a surprisingly low number of students per micro. 20,000 elementary schools have fewer than 60 students per micro; in fact 8,500 have fewer than 30 students per micro. Of course, secondary schools continue to have better (lower) density, since micros are often arrayed in large numbers in lab and media center settings.

**Number of Students per Micro**

| | Total* | Elementary | Jr. High | Sr. High |
|---|---|---|---|---|
| 1-29 | 16,943 | 8,538 | 2,906 | 4,969 |
| 30-59 | 20,200 | 11,697 | 3,740 | 4,558 |
| 60-189 | 10,563 | 6,965 | 1,665 | 1,819 |
| 90-119 | 6,199 | 4,320 | 949 | 874 |
| 120-149 | 3,828 | 2,759 | 528 | 498 |
| 150-199 | 4,163 | 3,181 | 525 | 425 |
| 200-299 | 4,302 | 3,283 | 545 | 433 |
| 300+ | 6,471 | 4,555 | 972 | 868 |
| Uncl. | 1,710 | 1,031 | 124 | 240 |
| Total | 74,379 | 46,329 | 11,954 | 14,684 |

*Includes Other Special Grade Levels

For further information, including counts by state, contact Quality Education Data at 1-800-525-5811.

MICROPR 02/26/86

QUALITY EDUCATION DATA, INC.
A REPORT ON LARGE DISTRICT USE OF MICROCOMPUTERS
(IN ORDER BY DISTRICT NAME)

| DISTRICT NAME | ST | TOTAL MICROS | TOTAL STUDENTS | TOTAL SCHOOLS | APPLE | R.S. | COMM. | T.I. | ATARI | IBM | FRANK | OTHER | MICROS PER SCH |
|---|---|---|---|---|---|---|---|---|---|---|---|---|---|
| ADAMS-ARAPAHOE DIST 28J | CO | 620 | 26000 | 43 | 560 | 0 | 30 | 30 | 0 | 0 | 0 | 0 | 14 |
| AKRON CITY SCHOOL DISTRICT | OH | 375 | 35596 | 58 | 345 | 15 | 15 | 0 | 0 | 0 | 0 | 0 | 6 |
| ALBUQUERQUE SCHOOL DISTRICT | NM | 2811 | 71555 | 112 | 2170 | 0 | 0 | 0 | 0 | 514 | 0 | 127 | 25 |
| ALDINE INDEP SCHOOL DISTRICT | TX | 764 | 36000 | 33 | 305 | 10 | 446 | 0 | 0 | 3 | 0 | 0 | 23 |
| ALPINE SCHOOL DISTRICT | UT | 834 | 33948 | 48 | 311 | 0 | 356 | 0 | 0 | 132 | 0 | 35 | 17 |
| AMARILLO INDEP SCH DIST | TX | 242 | 27688 | 47 | 242 | 0 | 0 | 0 | 0 | 0 | 0 | 0 | 5 |
| ANCHORAGE SCHOOL DISTRICT | AK | 2342 | 42406 | 70 | 2300 | 0 | 0 | 0 | 0 | 6 | 0 | 36 | 33 |
| ANNE ARUNDEL CO SCH DISTRICT | MD | 872 | 62622 | 119 | 221 | 244 | 407 | 0 | 0 | 0 | 0 | 0 | 7 |
| ANOKA HENNEPIN SCHOOL DISTRICT | MN | 393 | 31040 | 35 | 300 | 62 | 1 | 0 | 0 | 30 | 0 | 0 | 11 |
| ARLINGTON INDEP SCHOOL DIST | TX | 1002 | 36680 | 45 | 20 | 0 | 682 | 0 | 0 | 0 | 0 | 300 | 22 |
| ATLANTA PUBLIC SCHOOL DISTRICT | GA | 1051 | 66121 | 117 | 378 | 81 | 132 | 0 | 0 | 0 | 0 | 460 | 9 |
| AUSTIN INDEP SCHOOL DIST | TX | 1925 | 58155 | 82 | 700 | 0 | 0 | 368 | 0 | 300 | 0 | 557 | 23 |
| BALTIMORE CITY SCHOOL DISTRICT | MD | 937 | 113500 | 195 | 450 | 300 | 12 | 0 | 0 | 175 | 0 | 0 | 5 |
| BALTIMORE COUNTY SCHOOL DIST | MD | 2211 | 80854 | 147 | 961 | 200 | 50 | 1000 | 0 | 0 | 0 | 0 | 15 |
| BIBB CO SCHOOL DISTRICT | GA | 198 | 25056 | 41 | 165 | 17 | 0 | 0 | 0 | 6 | 0 | 10 | 5 |
| BIRMINGHAM CITY SCHOOL DIST | AL | 530 | 45000 | 87 | 400 | 90 | 0 | 15 | 0 | 0 | 0 | 25 | 6 |
| BOSTON SCHOOL DISTRICT | MA | 3003 | 60000 | 126 | 992 | 0 | 0 | 0 | 0 | 1174 | 0 | 837 | 24 |
| BREVARD COUNTY SCHOOL DISTRICT | FL | 1892 | 46000 | 63 | 894 | 357 | 534 | 0 | 10 | 9 | 0 | 88 | 30 |
| BROWARD COUNTY SCHOOL DISTRICT | FL | 7062 | 126673 | 176 | 6397 | 0 | 0 | 0 | 0 | 589 | 0 | 76 | 40 |
| BROWNSVILLE INDEP SCH DIST | TX | 1290 | 31855 | 32 | 340 | 940 | 0 | 10 | 0 | 0 | 0 | 0 | 40 |

| DISTRICT NAME | ST | TOTAL MICROS | TOTAL STUDENTS | TOTAL SCHOOLS | APPLE | R.S. | COMM. | T.I. | ATARI | IBM | FRANK | OTHER | MICROS PER SCH |
|---|---|---|---|---|---|---|---|---|---|---|---|---|---|
| BUFFALO PUBLIC SCHOOL DISTRICT | NY | 640 | 46608 | 74 | 400 | 110 | 0 | 0 | 0 | 30 | 100 | 0 | 9 |
| CADDO PARISH SCHOOLS | LA | 532 | 46934 | 73 | 183 | 56 | 9 | 0 | 0 | 284 | 0 | 0 | 7 |
| CALCASIEU PARISH SCHOOL DIST | LA | 576 | 31893 | 59 | 56 | 350 | 54 | 0 | 0 | 36 | 0 | 80 | 10 |
| CHARLESTON COUNTY SCHOOL DIST | SC | 1776 | 42687 | 75 | 1257 | 185 | 0 | 0 | 0 | 334 | 0 | 0 | 24 |
| CHARLOTTE-MECKLENBURG DIST 30 | NC | 2750 | 72270 | 106 | 1300 | 1050 | 0 | 0 | 0 | 400 | 0 | 0 | 26 |
| CHERRY CREEK SCHOOL DISTRICT | CO | 1049 | 26000 | 33 | 1000 | 0 | 9 | 15 | 0 | 25 | 0 | 0 | 32 |
| CHESAPEAKE CITY SCHOOL DIST | VA | 177 | 25179 | 37 | 5 | 167 | 4 | 0 | 0 | 0 | 0 | 1 | 5 |
| CHESTERFIELD CO SCHOOL DIST | VA | 1110 | 36900 | 42 | 1100 | 0 | 0 | 0 | 10 | 0 | 0 | 0 | 26 |
| CHICAGO PUBLIC SCHOOLS | IL | 5916 | 431296 | 579 | 2318 | 908 | 790 | 0 | 0 | 0 | 0 | 1900 | 10 |
| CINCINNATI CITY SCH DIST | OH | 235 | 51244 | 92 | 175 | 0 | 0 | 50 | 10 | 0 | 0 | 0 | 3 |
| CLARK CO SCHOOL DISTRICT | NV | 1064 | 89752 | 119 | 355 | 0 | 355 | 354 | 0 | 0 | 0 | 0 | 9 |
| CLAYTON CO SCHOOL DISTRICT | GA | 600 | 33276 | 41 | 600 | 0 | 0 | 0 | 0 | 0 | 0 | 0 | 15 |
| CLEVELAND CITY SCH DIST | OH | 936 | 76227 | 128 | 18 | 61 | 0 | 0 | 0 | 820 | 0 | 37 | 7 |
| COBB COUNTY SCHOOL DISTRICT | GA | 1615 | 59000 | 73 | 1492 | 40 | 83 | 0 | 0 | 0 | 0 | 0 | 22 |
| COLORADO SPRINGS SCH DIST II | CO | 814 | 30125 | 50 | 800 | 0 | 2 | 0 | 0 | 1 | 0 | 11 | 16 |
| COLUMBUS CITY SCHOOL DISTRICT | OH | 1130 | 67647 | 129 | 1010 | 20 | 100 | 0 | 0 | 0 | 0 | 0 | 9 |
| COMPTON UNIF SCHOOL DISTRICT | CA | 235 | 26815 | 39 | 190 | 35 | 8 | 0 | 0 | 2 | 0 | 0 | 6 |
| CORPUS CHRISTI INDEP SCH DIST | TX | 946 | 36895 | 57 | 495 | 350 | 0 | 12 | 0 | 0 | 89 | 0 | 17 |
| CUMBERLAND COUNTY SCH DIST | NC | 830 | 37236 | 54 | 100 | 110 | 0 | 20 | 0 | 600 | 0 | 0 | 15 |
| CYPRESS FAIRBANKS SCHOOL DIST | TX | 1090 | 32094 | 30 | 5 | 60 | 925 | 0 | 0 | 0 | 0 | 100 | 36 |

| DISTRICT NAME | ST | TOTAL MICROS | TOTAL STUDENTS | TOTAL SCHOOLS | APPLE | R.S. | COMM. | T.I. | ATARI | IBM | FRANK | OTHER | MICROS PER SCH |
|---|---|---|---|---|---|---|---|---|---|---|---|---|---|
| DADE COUNTY SCHOOL DISTRICT | FL | 4473 | 229866 | 254 | 1960 | 437 | 0 | 0 | 1393 | 683 | 0 | 0 | 18 |
| DALLAS INDEPENDENT SCH DIST | TX | 3000 | 128245 | 185 | 300 | 1200 | 1500 | 0 | 0 | 0 | 0 | 0 | 16 |
| DAVIS COUNTY SCHOOL DISTRICT | UT | 568 | 46547 | 65 | 506 | 2 | 0 | 0 | 0 | 60 | 0 | 0 | 9 |
| DAYTON CITY SCHOOL DISTRICT | OH | 332 | 30018 | 48 | 233 | 69 | 15 | 0 | 0 | 15 | 0 | 0 | 7 |
| DEKALB CO SCHOOL DISTRICT | GA | 2063 | 69140 | 106 | 1935 | 0 | 0 | 0 | 0 | 113 | 0 | 15 | 19 |
| DENVER SCHOOL DISTRICT I | CO | 1818 | 58271 | 113 | 916 | 0 | 761 | 0 | 0 | 0 | 0 | 141 | 16 |
| DES MOINES SCH DIST | IA | 432 | 30921 | 62 | 197 | 25 | 185 | 0 | 0 | 25 | 0 | 0 | 7 |
| DETROIT PUBLIC SCHOOL DISTRICT | MI | 3000 | 192464 | 277 | 2700 | 0 | 0 | 0 | 0 | 300 | 0 | 0 | 11 |
| DISTRICT OF COLUMBIA SCH DIST | DC | 2131 | 87927 | 188 | 0 | 0 | 587 | 0 | 0 | 764 | 0 | 780 | 11 |
| DUVAL CO SCHOOL DISTRICT | FL | 2666 | 100132 | 143 | 73 | 2593 | 0 | 0 | 0 | 0 | 0 | 0 | 19 |
| EAST BATON ROUGE PARISH DIST | LA | 689 | 54875 | 104 | 84 | 66 | 0 | 0 | 83 | 0 | 456 | 0 | 7 |
| EL PASO INDEP SCHOOL DISTRICT | TX | 719 | 59510 | 70 | 645 | 0 | 10 | 0 | 0 | 0 | 0 | 64 | 10 |
| ELGIN SCHOOL DISTRICT | IL | 207 | 25611 | 41 | 198 | 6 | 0 | 0 | 0 | 0 | 0 | 3 | 5 |
| ESCAMBIA CO SCHOOL DISTRICT | FL | 288 | 39677 | 59 | 130 | 92 | 50 | 0 | 0 | 0 | 0 | 16 | 5 |
| FAIRFAX COUNTY SCHOOL DISTRICT | VA | 2280 | 126206 | 162 | 159 | 0 | 0 | 0 | 1599 | 79 | 0 | 443 | 14 |
| FAYETTE CO SCHOOL DISTRICT | KY | 481 | 30129 | 48 | 69 | 0 | 0 | 8 | 63 | 0 | 0 | 341 | 10 |
| FLINT COMM SCHOOL DISTRICT | MI | 278 | 33676 | 52 | 32 | 44 | 0 | 0 | 112 | 90 | 0 | 0 | 5 |
| FORT BEND INDEP SCH DIST | TX | 360 | 25500 | 28 | 350 | 0 | 0 | 10 | 0 | 0 | 0 | 0 | 13 |
| FORT WAYNE SCHOOL DISTRICT | IN | 1635 | 32175 | 53 | 1445 | 0 | 0 | 0 | 0 | 120 | 0 | 70 | 31 |
| FORT WORTH INDEP SCH DIST | TX | 1350 | 67373 | 98 | 150 | 1200 | 0 | 0 | 0 | 0 | 0 | 0 | 14 |

| DISTRICT NAME | ST | TOTAL MICROS | TOTAL STUDENTS | TOTAL SCHOOLS | APPLE | R.S. | COMM. | T.I. | ATARI | IBM | FRANK | OTHER | MICROS PER SCH |
|---|---|---|---|---|---|---|---|---|---|---|---|---|---|
| FRESNO UN SCH DIST | CA | 955 | 49137 | 85 | 500 | 242 | 0 | 28 | 0 | 185 | 0 | 0 | 11 |
| FULTON CO SCHOOL DISTRICT | GA | 877 | 37000 | 75 | 572 | 3 | 0 | 0 | 0 | 300 | 0 | 2 | 12 |
| GARDEN GROVE UN SCH DIST | CA | 335 | 36700 | 57 | 300 | 20 | 15 | 0 | 0 | 0 | 0 | 0 | 6 |
| GARLAND INDEP SCHOOL DISTRICT | TX | 188 | 31489 | 50 | 45 | 45 | 10 | 0 | 0 | 0 | 0 | 88 | 4 |
| GARY COMM SCHOOL CORP | IN | 848 | 28032 | 42 | 354 | 27 | 467 | 0 | 0 | 0 | 0 | 0 | 20 |
| GASTON CO SCH DIST | NC | 266 | 31277 | 56 | 36 | 228 | 0 | 0 | 0 | 0 | 0 | 2 | 5 |
| GRAND RAPIDS SCHOOL DISTRICT | MI | 262 | 32244 | 56 | 68 | 111 | 78 | 0 | 0 | 0 | 0 | 5 | 5 |
| GRANITE SCHOOL DISTRICT | UT | 1270 | 69930 | 90 | 100 | 0 | 50 | 0 | 860 | 260 | 0 | 0 | 14 |
| GREENVILLE CO SCHOOL DISTRICT | SC | 1028 | 51500 | 104 | 856 | 38 | 0 | 0 | 58 | 0 | 0 | 76 | 10 |
| GWINNETT CO SCHOOL DISTRICT | GA | 632 | 44734 | 51 | 616 | 6 | 0 | 0 | 0 | 0 | 0 | 10 | 12 |
| HARFORD COUNTY SCHOOL DIST | MD | 272 | 27445 | 42 | 198 | 0 | 6 | 0 | 0 | 68 | 0 | 0 | 6 |
| HAWAII DEPT OF EDUCATION | HI | 1993 | 171000 | 243 | 1193 | 380 | 171 | 0 | 0 | 249 | 0 | 0 | 8 |
| HENRICO CO SCHOOL DISTRICT | VA | 956 | 30590 | 51 | 536 | 162 | 10 | 5 | 5 | 1 | 145 | 92 | 19 |
| HILLSBOROUGH COUNTY SCH DIST | FL | 1840 | 112000 | 132 | 286 | 839 | 0 | 0 | 677 | 38 | 0 | 0 | 14 |
| HOUSTON INDEP SCH DISTRICT | TX | 6150 | 187031 | 217 | 4500 | 500 | 0 | 0 | 0 | 150 | 1000 | 0 | 28 |
| HUNTSVILLE CITY SCHOOL DIST | AL | 567 | 25438 | 40 | 62 | 0 | 0 | 0 | 28 | 336 | 0 | 141 | 14 |
| INDIANAPOLIS SCHOOL DISTRICT | IN | 1787 | 54070 | 85 | 655 | 0 | 93 | 0 | 0 | 1025 | 0 | 14 | 21 |
| JACKSON SCHOOL DISTRICT | MS | 456 | 29380 | 57 | 12 | 0 | 0 | 0 | 0 | 444 | 0 | 0 | 8 |
| JEFFCO SCHOOL DISTRICT RI | CO | 2576 | 75785 | 112 | 2400 | 0 | 62 | 0 | 0 | 75 | 0 | 39 | 23 |
| JEFFERSON CO BOARD OF ED | AL | 980 | 46000 | 75 | 662 | 285 | 13 | 0 | 0 | 0 | 0 | 20 | 13 |

| DISTRICT NAME | ST | TOTAL MICROS | TOTAL STUDENTS | TOTAL SCHOOLS | APPLE | R.S. | COMM. | T.I. | ATARI | IBM | FRANK | OTHER | MICROS PER SCH |
|---|---|---|---|---|---|---|---|---|---|---|---|---|---|
| JEFFERSON CO PUBLIC SCHOOLS | KY | 2851 | 92566 | 153 | 1606 | 0 | 750 | 0 | 0 | 245 | 0 | 250 | 19 |
| JEFFERSON PARISH | LA | 200 | 59807 | 84 | 55 | 145 | 0 | 0 | 0 | 0 | 0 | 0 | 2 |
| JERSEY CITY SCHOOL DISTRICT | NJ | 1207 | 29957 | 35 | 792 | 151 | 264 | 0 | 0 | 0 | 0 | 0 | 34 |
| JORDAN SCHOOL DISTRICT | UT | 777 | 58643 | 65 | 318 | 3 | 81 | 36 | 102 | 48 | 186 | 3 | 12 |
| KANAWHA COUNTY SCHOOLS | WV | 1144 | 39131 | 115 | 135 | 0 | 0 | 0 | 300 | 158 | 0 | 551 | 10 |
| KANSAS CITY SCHOOL DISTRICT | MO | 385 | 35929 | 70 | 55 | 300 | 27 | 0 | 0 | 3 | 0 | 0 | 6 |
| KNOX CO DISTRICT | TN | 467 | 26387 | 41 | 154 | 265 | 40 | 0 | 0 | 0 | 0 | 8 | 11 |
| LAFAYETTE PARISH SCHOOL DIST | LA | 210 | 27088 | 40 | 69 | 89 | 6 | 0 | 0 | 0 | 0 | 46 | 5 |
| LEE COUNTY SCHOOL DISTRICT | FL | 632 | 32100 | 48 | 400 | 152 | 9 | 0 | 0 | 0 | 0 | 71 | 13 |
| LONG BEACH UNIF SCH DIST | CA | 450 | 60431 | 79 | 300 | 140 | 0 | 0 | 0 | 10 | 0 | 0 | 6 |
| LOS ANGELES CITY SCHOOLS | CA | 3226 | 698107 | 751 | 1426 | 127 | 418 | 15 | 0 | 1000 | 0 | 240 | 4 |
| LUBBOCK INDEP SCHOOL DISTRICT | TX | 1089 | 26787 | 56 | 598 | 20 | 0 | 225 | 0 | 30 | 0 | 216 | 19 |
| MARION COUNTY SCHOOL DISTRICT | FL | 959 | 25000 | 33 | 100 | 250 | 0 | 0 | 9 | 600 | 0 | 0 | 29 |
| MEMPHIS CITY SCH DIST | TN | 3311 | 107000 | 159 | 1500 | 0 | 0 | 1200 | 0 | 150 | 461 | 0 | 21 |
| MESA UNIF SCHOOL DISTRICT | AZ | 484 | 46688 | 51 | 8 | 0 | 433 | 0 | 0 | 26 | 17 | 0 | 9 |
| METROPOLITAN SCHOOL DISTRICT | TN | 792 | 63700 | 119 | 600 | 190 | 1 | 0 | 0 | 1 | 0 | 0 | 7 |
| MILWAUKEE SCHOOL DISTRICT | WI | 1311 | 87624 | 143 | 1100 | 0 | 0 | 5 | 0 | 76 | 0 | 130 | 9 |
| MINNEAPOLIS SCHOOL DISTRICT | MN | 1100 | 38483 | 55 | 1000 | 0 | 0 | 0 | 0 | 100 | 0 | 0 | 20 |
| MOBILE COUNTY SCHOOL DISTRICT | AL | 558 | 68103 | 87 | 370 | 33 | 81 | 0 | 0 | 74 | 0 | 0 | 6 |
| MONTEBELLO UNIF SCHOOL DIST | CA | 415 | 29319 | 47 | 400 | 0 | 0 | 0 | 0 | 15 | 0 | 0 | 9 |

| DISTRICT NAME | ST | TOTAL MICROS | TOTAL STUDENTS | TOTAL SCHOOLS | APPLE | R.S. | COMM. | T.I. | ATARI | IBM | FRANK | OTHER | MICROS PER SCH |
|---|---|---|---|---|---|---|---|---|---|---|---|---|---|
| MONTGOMERY COUNTY SCH DIST | MD | 3074 | 91704 | 155 | 2434 | 0 | 600 | 0 | 0 | 40 | 0 | 0 | 20 |
| MONTGOMERY COUNTY SCHOOL DIST | AL | 468 | 35556 | 52 | 303 | 151 | 2 | 0 | 0 | 0 | 0 | 12 | 9 |
| MT DIABLO UNIF SCHOOL DISTRICT | CA | 774 | 31957 | 45 | 298 | 0 | 334 | 0 | 0 | 13 | 0 | 129 | 17 |
| MUSCOGEE CO SCHOOL DISTRICT | GA | 235 | 30681 | 56 | 233 | 0 | 0 | 0 | 0 | 0 | 0 | 2 | 4 |
| NEW YORK CITY SCHOOLS | NY | 8000 | 950384 | 998 | 2000 | 2000 | 2500 | 1500 | 0 | 0 | 0 | 0 | 8 |
| NEWARK SCHOOL DISTRICT | NJ | 585 | 55116 | 83 | 58 | 0 | 87 | 0 | 0 | 440 | 0 | 0 | 7 |
| NORFOLK SCHOOL DISTRICT | VA | 538 | 35540 | 58 | 235 | 0 | 0 | 0 | 0 | 275 | 0 | 28 | 9 |
| NORTHEAST INDEP SCH DIST | TX | 740 | 36881 | 39 | 364 | 0 | 254 | 0 | 0 | 4 | 0 | 118 | 19 |
| NORTHSIDE ISD | TX | 332 | 40768 | 49 | 118 | 99 | 0 | 0 | 0 | 82 | 0 | 33 | 7 |
| OAKLAND CITY UNIF SCH DIST | CA | 1064 | 50955 | 96 | 295 | 252 | 407 | 0 | 0 | 110 | 0 | 0 | 11 |
| OKLAHOMA CITY SCHOOL DISTRICT | OK | 624 | 43000 | 92 | 152 | 310 | 162 | 0 | 0 | 0 | 0 | 0 | 7 |
| OMAHA PUBLIC SCHOOL DISTRICT | NE | 1161 | 41229 | 80 | 1000 | 126 | 0 | 0 | 0 | 0 | 15 | 20 | 15 |
| ORANGE COUNTY SCHOOL DISTRICT | FL | 1979 | 80039 | 104 | 1156 | 767 | 0 | 0 | 0 | 35 | 0 | 21 | 19 |
| ORANGE UNIF SCHOOL DISTRICT | CA | 511 | 25000 | 37 | 465 | 1 | 22 | 12 | 0 | 1 | 7 | 3 | 14 |
| ORLEANS PARISH SCHOOLS | LA | 549 | 83820 | 140 | 137 | 142 | 121 | 0 | 0 | 0 | 0 | 149 | 4 |
| PALM BEACH CO SCHOOL DISTRICT | FL | 980 | 75023 | 96 | 50 | 180 | 0 | 0 | 0 | 750 | 0 | 0 | 10 |
| PASADENA INDEP SCHOOL DISTRICT | TX | 400 | 35826 | 44 | 400 | 0 | 0 | 0 | 0 | 0 | 0 | 0 | 9 |
| PASCO CO SCH DIST | FL | 655 | 28551 | 34 | 500 | 100 | 0 | 0 | 0 | 35 | 0 | 20 | 19 |
| PATERSON SCHOOL DISTRICT | NJ | 117 | 25000 | 32 | 49 | 0 | 60 | 0 | 0 | 8 | 0 | 0 | 4 |
| PHILADELPHIA SCHOOL DISTRICT | PA | 3085 | 198000 | 256 | 2400 | 356 | 244 | 0 | 0 | 85 | 0 | 0 | 12 |

| DISTRICT NAME | ST | TOTAL MICROS | TOTAL STUDENTS | TOTAL SCHOOLS | APPLE | R.S. | COMM. | T.I. | ATARI | IBM | FRANK | OTHER | MICROS PER SCH |
|---|---|---|---|---|---|---|---|---|---|---|---|---|---|
| PITTSBURG SCHOOL DISTRICT | PA | 642 | 40257 | 88 | 104 | 473 | 0 | 0 | 0 | 0 | 0 | 65 | 7 |
| PLANO INDEP SCHOOL DISTRICT | TX | 1541 | 26789 | 33 | 1200 | 0 | 0 | 0 | 0 | 208 | 43 | 90 | 47 |
| POLK CO SCHOOL DISTRICT | FL | 2151 | 57207 | 104 | 403 | 969 | 672 | 0 | 0 | 107 | 0 | 0 | 21 |
| PORTLAND SCHOOL DISTRICT | OR | 2324 | 51003 | 92 | 1216 | 452 | 104 | 0 | 0 | 479 | 0 | 73 | 25 |
| PRINCE GEORGES CO SCH DIST | MD | 890 | 103684 | 180 | 123 | 358 | 354 | 55 | 0 | 0 | 0 | 0 | 5 |
| PRINCE WILLIAM COUNTY SCH DIST | VA | 403 | 36757 | 52 | 397 | 6 | 0 | 0 | 0 | 0 | 0 | 0 | 8 |
| PULASKI CO SPEC SCHOOL DIST | AR | 618 | 30240 | 50 | 75 | 57 | 174 | 13 | 0 | 0 | 3 | 296 | 12 |
| RICHARDSON INDEP SCHOOL DIST | TX | 970 | 33377 | 48 | 886 | 0 | 0 | 80 | 0 | 2 | 0 | 2 | 20 |
| RICHLAND CO SCH DIST | SC | 262 | 27959 | 49 | 124 | 95 | 3 | 0 | 0 | 40 | 0 | 0 | 5 |
| RICHMOND CITY SCHOOL DISTRICT | VA | 646 | 29350 | 59 | 525 | 80 | 0 | 0 | 1 | 0 | 0 | 40 | 11 |
| RICHMOND COUNTY SCHOOL DIST | GA | 419 | 31696 | 52 | 280 | 48 | 19 | 0 | 15 | 0 | 0 | 57 | 8 |
| RICHMOND UNIF SCH DIST | CA | 353 | 25662 | 58 | 276 | 10 | 37 | 0 | 0 | 0 | 0 | 30 | 6 |
| RIVERSIDE UNIF SCHOOL DISTRICT | CA | 143 | 26411 | 35 | 87 | 50 | 1 | 0 | 0 | 0 | 0 | 5 | 4 |
| ROCHESTER CITY SCHOOL DISTRICT | NY | 1153 | 32625 | 53 | 505 | 391 | 160 | 0 | 0 | 32 | 0 | 65 | 22 |
| ROCKFORD BOARD OF EDUCATION | IL | 1371 | 29000 | 54 | 150 | 505 | 706 | 0 | 0 | 0 | 0 | 10 | 25 |
| SACRAMENTO CITY UNIF SCH DIST | CA | 540 | 47678 | 76 | 315 | 142 | 45 | 0 | 0 | 0 | 0 | 38 | 7 |
| SAN ANTONIO INDEP SCH DIST | TX | 1704 | 66322 | 70 | 100 | 1300 | 0 | 0 | 0 | 0 | 0 | 304 | 24 |
| SAN BERNARDINO UN SCH DIST | CA | 207 | 29993 | 50 | 174 | 22 | 0 | 0 | 0 | 0 | 8 | 3 | 4 |
| SAN DIEGO SCHOOL DISTRICT | CA | 2266 | 111349 | 182 | 2266 | 0 | 0 | 0 | 0 | 0 | 0 | 0 | 12 |
| SAN FRANCISCO UNIF SCH DIST | CA | 1477 | 64734 | 132 | 912 | 143 | 48 | 66 | 140 | 111 | 0 | 57 | 11 |

| DISTRICT NAME | ST | TOTAL MICROS | TOTAL STUDENTS | TOTAL SCHOOLS | APPLE | R.S. | COMM. | T.I. | ATARI | IBM | FRANK | OTHER | MICROS PER SCH |
|---|---|---|---|---|---|---|---|---|---|---|---|---|---|
| SAN JOSE UNIF SCH DIST | CA | 308 | 31115 | 19 | 275 | 1 | 2 | 0 | 0 | 30 | 0 | 0 | 16 |
| SAN JUAN UNIF SCHOOL DISTRICT | CA | 1206 | 42429 | 73 | 600 | 316 | 64 | 1 | 28 | 79 | 8 | 110 | 17 |
| SANTA ANA UNIF SCHOOL DISTRICT | CA | 171 | 35265 | 40 | 150 | 21 | 0 | 0 | 0 | 0 | 0 | 0 | 4 |
| SARASOTA COUNTY SCHOOL DIST | FL | 566 | 25000 | 34 | 361 | 68 | 0 | 0 | 0 | 103 | 0 | 34 | 17 |
| SAVANNAH-CHATHAM CO SCH DIST | GA | 294 | 29936 | 53 | 27 | 17 | 250 | 0 | 0 | 0 | 0 | 0 | 6 |
| SCHOOL BOARD OF PINELLAS CO | FL | 500 | 95187 | 112 | 470 | 30 | 0 | 0 | 0 | 0 | 0 | 0 | 4 |
| SEATTLE SCH DIST | WA | 1085 | 43676 | 93 | 450 | 155 | 420 | 0 | 0 | 60 | 0 | 0 | 12 |
| SEMINOLE COUNTY SCHOOL DIST | FL | 660 | 38534 | 40 | 446 | 188 | 0 | 6 | 0 | 20 | 0 | 0 | 16 |
| SHAWNEE MISSION DISTRICT 512 | KS | 722 | 30014 | 56 | 717 | 1 | 0 | 0 | 0 | 1 | 0 | 3 | 13 |
| SHELBY COUNTY SCHOOL DISTRICT | TN | 659 | 30000 | 34 | 448 | 175 | 0 | 21 | 0 | 0 | 0 | 15 | 19 |
| SPOKANE SCHOOL DISTRICT | WA | 900 | 27341 | 52 | 900 | 0 | 0 | 0 | 0 | 0 | 0 | 0 | 17 |
| SPRING BRANCH SCHOOL DISTRICT | TX | 1237 | 25000 | 35 | 828 | 40 | 275 | 0 | 0 | 0 | 0 | 94 | 35 |
| ST LOUIS CITY SCHOOL DISTRICT | MO | 1079 | 51253 | 122 | 207 | 0 | 124 | 0 | 0 | 662 | 0 | 86 | 9 |
| ST PAUL INDEP SCHOOL DISTRICT | MN | 1158 | 30654 | 56 | 1138 | 0 | 0 | 0 | 20 | 0 | 0 | 0 | 21 |
| STOCKTON UNIF SCHOOL DISTRICT | CA | 250 | 25872 | 45 | 129 | 23 | 75 | 0 | 0 | 0 | 0 | 23 | 6 |
| TACOMA SCHOOL DISTRICT | WA | 590 | 26500 | 57 | 570 | 10 | 0 | 0 | 0 | 10 | 0 | 0 | 10 |
| TOLEDO SCHOOL DISTRICT | OH | 104 | 42467 | 63 | 0 | 0 | 42 | 14 | 0 | 48 | 0 | 0 | 2 |
| TUCSON UN SCH DIST | AZ | 1538 | 53230 | 101 | 848 | 159 | 220 | 25 | 2 | 163 | 0 | 121 | 15 |
| TULSA INDEP SCHOOL DISTRICT | OK | 1851 | 44067 | 89 | 1500 | 224 | 35 | 0 | 0 | 92 | 0 | 0 | 21 |
| VIRGINIA BEACH CITY SCH DIST | VA | 826 | 60000 | 63 | 556 | 150 | 0 | 0 | 0 | 120 | 0 | 0 | 13 |

| DISTRICT NAME | ST | TOTAL MICROS | TOTAL STUDENTS | TOTAL SCHOOLS | APPLE | R.S. | COMM. | T.I. | ATARI | IBM | FRANK | OTHER | MICROS PER SCH |
|---|---|---|---|---|---|---|---|---|---|---|---|---|---|
| VOLUSIA CO SCHOOL DISTRICT | FL | 630 | 36658 | 50 | 284 | 310 | 26 | 0 | 0 | 10 | 0 | 0 | 13 |
| WAKE COUNTY SCHOOL DISTRICT | NC | 787 | 54019 | 78 | 483 | 0 | 0 | 0 | 0 | 304 | 0 | 0 | 10 |
| WASHOE COUNTY SCHOOL DISTRICT | NV | 1320 | 32272 | 60 | 370 | 455 | 70 | 0 | 0 | 0 | 425 | 0 | 22 |
| WICHITA UNIFIED SCH DIST 259 | KS | 1066 | 43270 | 111 | 1050 | 3 | 0 | 0 | 0 | 13 | 0 | 0 | 10 |
| WINSTON-SALEM FORSYTH CO DIST | NC | 696 | 39228 | 54 | 645 | 14 | 35 | 2 | 0 | 0 | 0 | 0 | 13 |
| YSLETA INDEP SCH DIST | TX | 819 | 47611 | 46 | 460 | 5 | 287 | 0 | 0 | 0 | 0 | 67 | 18 |
| *** Total *** | | 195924 | 10586443 | 15372 | 105006 | 28253 | 20238 | 5201 | 5525 | 17958 | 2963 | 10780 | |

# *Enrollment Differences in Computer Camps and Summer Classes*

**by Irene T. Miura and Robert D. Hess**

*Irene T. Miura and Robert D. Hess are at the Stanford University School of Education, California.*

If sex and socioeconomic status (SES) inequities exist in computer training during the school years, they threaten recent attempts to adjust traditional inequities in access to education and employment. Are there differences by gender and SES in enrollment in summer camps and classes, a form of personal computer use that is to some degree voluntary and that involves courses designed to teach programming and other technical aspects of computer use?

## METHOD

The data were gathered by a one-page questionnaire from directors of summer computer camps and classes. The data came from 5,533 students in approximately 132 different instructional groups, conducted by 23 different sponsors (66% response). The analysis focused on enrollment by grade, sex, SES, and ethnic origin, as well as the type of sponsorship (private, university or public school), cost and residential versus day camp accommodations.

## RESULTS

The analysis of data was oriented around three questions:

1. Do more boys than girls enroll in summer computer camps and classes?
2. Does the ratio of boys to girls vary by grade level?
3. Does the ratio vary by sponsorship, cost and accommodation?

In addition, a summary of information about SES and ethnic background of the students was made.

The ratio of boys to girls is roughly three to one (74% boys to 26% girls). For the total group, sex differences were related to grade level, cost of the sessions, type of sponsorship and accommodation. The proportion of girls is highest in day classes sponsored by the public schools and lowest in private residential camps. The trends

Reprinted with permission from *The Computing Teacher*, April 1984, vol. 11, no. 8. Published by the International Council for Computers in Education.

in gender differences by cost and grade level were also statistically significant. The proportion of girls decreased as cost and grade level increased.

Differential enrollment was even more striking when tallied by level of course offering. Three programs (student N=559) categorized courses by level of difficulty. The proportion of females enrolled in beginning and intermediate classes was 28%; in advanced programming classes it was 14%; only 5% of those enrolled in the more advanced assembly language courses were female.

Directors reported that students were predominantly middle and upper income (98%). In addition, enrollment was overwhelmingly Caucasian. Ninety-one percent of the students were described as Caucasian, with Asians 5%, Blacks 2.5%, Hispanics 1% and Native Americans 0.5%.

## CONCLUSIONS

We conclude from these results that training in computer programming outside of course offerings during the school year is sought more often by males and by children and adolescents from middle and upper income families. Moreover, the disparity between boys and girls increases with age, is greater in advanced than in beginning classes, and is larger for expensive programs.

These disparities in computer literacy obviously have theoretical and social importance. The social significance follows from economic and educational opportunities open to students who have computer knowledge. These differences in the tendency to acquire programming skills may be expected to increase gender and socio-ethnic inequities that now exist in the labor market. The extent of such advantage in career opportunities is not yet known, but economic projections of the growth of technologies that will utilize such skills suggest that it will be very large. The new technologies may threaten gains in educational and career opportunities for women and minorities that have been achieved at great effort in the past two decades.

The theoretical importance suggests the need to analyze the social and psychological processes that contribute to these differences in computer literacy in an effort to develop effective teaching strategies. Intervention by schools and other public agencies may be needed to prevent these inequities from becoming even more deeply ingrained into the society.

# *Do Your School Policies Provide Equal Access to Computers? Are You Sure?*

**by Phyllis A. DuBois and Jane G. Schubert**

*Phyllis A. DuBois is Associate Research Scientist, and Jane G. Schubert is Principal Research Scientist and Director, Center for Educational Equity, American Institutes for Research, Palo Alto, California.*

Research indicates that inequities exist in computer access and learning. Some of the inequities are well known: (1) students in wealthy schools have more access to computers than students in poor schools; the ratio of students to computers is 54:1 in the wealthiest districts and 73:1 in the poorest schools (Marketing Data Retrieval 1985); (2) disadvantaged students spend most of their computer time on drill-and-practice exercises (Becker 1983) rather than on programming or other problem-solving activities; and (3) more males than females attend private computer camps and take summer computer courses (Miura and Hess 1983).

The American Institutes for Research investigated the circumstances within schools that impede computer access and use. We collected 327 "critical incidents": descriptions of situations that educators and students in grades one through nine experienced in relation to computers. We obtained information about the participants in each incident, the circumstances, the immediate effects, and the long-term implications. We sorted the incidents to identify patterns, created a taxonomy, and derived a list of the positive and negative results of computer use and access. Our study uncovered some inequities that are not necessarily determined by economics or gender, but are the unintentional results of administrative actions.

## WHAT ADMINISTRATIVE ACTIONS CAUSE INEQUITIES?

We found four areas in which administrators or educational leaders set policies that *unintentionally* cause inequities in computer learning.

1. *Establishing irrelevant prerequisities to computer learning*. An incident from our study illustrates that criteria established for use of computers are sometimes inappropriate.

> At mid-year, a second grade boy had not yet been allowed to use the computer in his classroom. The teacher's requirement was that students had to be reading at grade level or higher to use the computer. Because

From *Educational Leadership* (March 1986): 41–44. Reprinted with permission of the Association for Supervision and Curriculum Development. 

the boy's reading level was not improving very rapidly, it seemed unlikely that he would get to use the computer at all during that school year.

We encountered a number of schools in which math scores determined who was allowed to take computer courses. In one elementary school, we found that students could use the computers only after they had finished their classroom assignments. Most of the boys sped through their work, then raced to the computers; some of the girls, more concerned with neatness and detail, never finished while computers were still available.

In each of these situations, a teacher's rule or a school policy established "gates" to computer learning that unfairly excluded students. For some of the students—the poor reader, the math phobic, the detail-oriented worker—the computer might be a tool that increases their motivation and improves their skills. While it is clear that we have more students than computers and must provide time for instruction that is not computer-centered, our prerequisites must be defensible. We need to ask: Who is being kept away from computers and why? Are our prerequisites valid and fair?

2. *Placing computers in inappropriate areas, limiting or precluding access for some students*. In elementary schools, computers are often placed in each classroom, regardless of the teacher's preparation for or willingness to use computers. In one classroom we visited, the computer was used almost continuously, including lunch period and before and after school. In another classroom, the teacher made no provision for computer activities, and the computer was almost never used.

In a junior high school, we found that all of the computers were in a math teacher's classroom, so only that teacher and his students could use the computers. Again students were kept away from computers as a result of administrative actions that led to unintended disparities. The questions here are: What is the purpose for locating computers in a specific area or class? Does the location of the computers make them available to as many students as possible?

3. *Overlooking staff members' reluctance or inability to provide computer instruction and supervision*. An elementary school teacher took her class to the computer lab three times a week when the computer teacher was there. When the computer teacher was absent for two weeks, the students had no computer work because the classroom teacher was afraid she would be unable to answer a request for assistance and would look foolish.

We also found that some teachers ignored the computers in their rooms out of fear, resentment, or indifference, and they conveyed a message to their students that computers are to be feared, mistrusted, and ignored. Situations that preclude student use of computers because of teacher ignorance seem intolerable. The questions here are: What attitudes are educators conveying? How are they using this tool? How can school administrators ensure "teacher readiness" for computer use?

4. *Accepting common assumptions about equitable computer learning*. Teachers at a junior high school chose six to eight 8th grade tutors each year. They selected only boys, who were "more knowledgeable and responsible." They never even considered asking girls. Because of the boys' experience and eagerness, the teachers relied on them, giving them even more experience while denying experience to the girls.

We observed programming classes dominated by boys and were told that the girls were "not interested." We learned of computer clubs dominated by males and were told that females did not want to join. We saw computer labs where males hurried in to grab the available computers, leaving females to wait for another day—or give up trying. Administrators, like teachers and parents, often accept computers as part of the male domain and attribute a lack of involvement on the part of females or other groups to disinterest when, in fact, the opportunity is not there or the activity is uninteresting. The computer itself *does* interest students, and it is neutral, requiring no "masculine" or "feminine" skills.

Here we should ask: Why are some students—females, limited-English-speaking students, average students, gifted students—not participating in computer class or activities? Is the computer used as a multipurpose tool that can serve individual interests?

## WHAT EDUCATORS CAN DO

Administrators and teachers can focus on five specific areas to ensure equitable access to computers:

1. *Find out more*. Our study resulted in the development of *IDEAS for Equitable Computer Learning*, which includes strategies that the educator-members of our advisory work group designed or had already applied. This resource is available from the Center for Educational Equity, American Institutes for Research, Box 1113, Palo Alto, CA 94302, for $8.75 including postage. The Center for Educational Equity is the Title IV Sex Desegregation Center for Arizona, California, and Nevada, and also offers staff development training in computer equity, as do many of the Title IV centers, for other areas.

Other resources include a packet of 50 strategies for schools, parents, and communities called *The Neuter Computer: Why and How to Encourage Computer Equity for Girls* from Computer Equity Training Project, Women's Action Alliance, 370 Lexington Avenue, New York, NY 10017, and a kit, *Programming Equity into Computer Education* ($9.95, prepaid), from PEER, 1413 K Street, N.W., Washington, DC 20005.

2. *Look at your prerequisities, computer locations, and staff qualifications and assumptions*. Some schools limit computer access to certain grades but include every student in that grade. Other schools limit computer use to one subject area and select a discipline, such as social studies, that does not evoke anxiety or disqualify students, as mathematics can. To encourage teachers to learn to use computers, some schools offer staff training and allow teachers to take computers home during weekends and vacations. Computers in teacher lounges with appealing but simple-to-use software like The Print Shop can motivate staff members to learn to use computers. Some use peer learning strategies with teachers, matching experienced and inexperienced teachers so that they can try out strategies while practicing computer skills. All of these possibilities stress the need to examine assumptions and to deal with their consequences in creative ways.

3. *Provide a range of computer experiences for students*. Realizing that different students respond to different types of activities, some schools provide a kaleidoscope of computer activities: drill and practice, data management, spread sheets, word processing, simulations, problem solving, programming—a wide range in which no assumptions are made about which students will "like" or "do well" with which activities. By providing multidimensional activities and equal time for students, these schools maximize the opportunities for computer learning.

4. *Plan for equal access and use of computers*. Some schools that have found that females are reluctant to use computers before and after school when males are pre-

sent have designated an equal number of Boys' and Girls' Days in the computer lab. Though fewer girls than boys come to the lab initially, these schools tell us that once the practice is established, more girls begin to use the lab. Other schools have made efforts to encourage females to be leaders, appointing them in numbers equal to the males as computer tutors. Schools have also made special efforts to provide role models for all of their students by (1) inviting computer experts who are female or members of an ethnic group in addition to experts who are male; (2) recruiting female and male computer teachers who represent a range of ethnic backgrounds; and (3) obtaining bulletin board materials, computer software, and curriculum materials that are free of bias.

5. *Become aware of equity issues in general.* Few administrators and teachers intentionally deny learning opportunities to students; they simply have not considered the effects of their actions. We have found that once educators realize which behaviors result in disparate learning opportunities, they change their behavior and seldom revert to inequitable practices. Many schools provide a variety of workshops or seminars that raise consciousness of equity issues. Such activities include studying teacher-student interactions to ensure equal attention to both genders; looking at enrollment patterns to see if courses are gender-balanced; examining instructional materials to eliminate gender bias and misrepresentation; providing positive role models, female and male, to expand students' perceived possibilities; and encouraging all students to prepare for careers that interest and challenge them.

## AN OVERALL RELEVANCE

Computers offer a unique opportunity and challenge to educators. Because they are still "new machines," computers do not yet have a clearly established role in the curriculum. They are ubiquitous and interest in them is high, so people are willing to listen to ideas about access, prerequisities, types of activity, and assumptions. By addressing equity in the area of computer education, we can help staff members see the relevance of equity in other areas. For example, one of the barriers our study identified was "Dominance by one student over another during computer time." If teachers can implement strategies to ensure that students are not dominated during computer time, they can use the same strategies for activities away from the computer. By working toward equity in computer learning, they can become aware of ways to work toward it in other areas as well.

## REFERENCES

Becker, H. *School Uses of Microcomputers*. Issue #3. Baltimore: Johns Hopkins University, 1983.

Marketing Data Retrieval. Survey cited in *The New York Times*. "There's a Computer Gap And It's Growing Wider," August 4, 1985.

Miura, I., and R. D. Hess. "Sex Differences in Computer Access, Interest, and Usage." Paper presented at the annual meeting of the American Psychological Association, Anaheim, California, 1983.

Background research for this article was supported by the Women's Educational Equity Program, Grant No. G008303375.

# *Here's How You Can Help Girls Take Greater Advantage of School Computers*

**by Jo Shuchat Sanders**

*Jo Shuchat Sanders is Director of the Computer Equity Training Project at the Women's Action Alliance, New York.*

Which students take the greatest advantage of having access to computers? You guessed it: boys.

In the 1970s, we learned about math anxiety—or, as I prefer to call it, math avoidance. We gained an understanding of why girls are more likely than boys to drop out of mathematics classes and what we could do to prevent it. Then, in the first few years of the 1980s, we learned about sex segregation in our vocational education programs, and we took steps to increase cross-sex enrollment in such traditionally sex-segregated programs as cosmetology and welding.

Now, the hot topic on the school equity horizon is sex equity in computer use. School people are beginning to notice that although the classroom computer is sex-neutral in design, it is less so in use. Concern is growing that if girls continue to avoid the computer when they have a choice about it in school, they won't be able to compete for high-paying jobs in computer-related fields when they grow up. And in the meantime, they will miss out on important educational advantages while they still are in school.

Evidence of a gender gap in school computer use is increasing. Consider:

- In 1982, Marlaine Lockheed of the Educational Testing Service in Princeton, N.J., found that although 40 percent of the boys at Princeton High School said they used the computer in their free periods, only 8 percent of the girls said they did so.
- A 1981-82 survey conducted by EQUALS, an organization promoting mathematics, science, and computer study for girls, found that only 29 percent of the students enrolled in high school computer classes were girls.

  Surveys conducted in California, Maryland, and Michigan and reported by the Project on Equal Education Rights turned up remarkably similar results: In all three states, the number of boys enrolled in high school programming courses was nearly twice the number of girls enrolled.
- Studies of optional computer use in middle schools conducted by my own group, the Computer Equity Training Project (more about this later), showed that at the start of the term in schools we worked with nearly four-fifths (78 percent) of the students who took advantage of free-time computer use were boys.

---

- The pattern is the same in higher education: Of the computer and information science degrees awarded in the U.S. in 1981, women earned 33 percent of the bachelor's degrees, 23 percent of the master's and 10 percent of the doctorates.

And the computer gender gap is not limited to schools: Studies of home computer use and enrollment in summer computer camps show boys, once again, are doing most of the computing in these settings. As for adults, we studied the extent to which mass-circulation computer magazines reflect (and perhaps create) a male audience; another analysis showed that computer purchasers overwhelmingly are male.

Even though the computer gender gap is evident outside the school as well as inside, schools are in the best position to do something about it. And the first step is for board members to understand where the problem comes from.

## CAUSES OF THE GENDER GAP

The reasons girls don't use school computers as much as boys do are subtle. (School board members, administrators, and teachers certainly aren't hanging signs on the machines saying, ''No Girls Allowed.'') Our research has turned up approximately 30 possible culprits. The following factors surely are at the basis of the computer gender gap—during the middle school years especially:

1. The chicken-and-egg pattern: Girls consider computers unfeminine because they see mostly boys using them.
2. Girls stay out of the computer room because their girlfriends aren't there—an important social dynamic at the middle school age.
3. Schools often make computers available for optional use on a first-come, first-served basis, and boys, in their enthusiasm for the machines, aggressively capture the opportunities. (How many female hackers have *you* seen?)
4. Most girls find LOGO an interesting computer language, but most schools teach BASIC.
5. One student to each computer—the usual school arrangement—doesn't meet adolescent girls' needs for social interaction.

Several other suspected culprits might be confirmed by future research. Heading this list is the fact that computers most often are associated with mathematics, and we already know mathematics is identified with males. Also, girls seem to prefer purposeful activities, and many computer activities involve pointless game playing and random exploration of the computer's capabilities. A related factor could be the macho nature of much recreational and educational software. Many computer games and programs are based on win/lose, conflict situations and contain a great deal of violence that repels many girls (and some boys, too, for that matter).

In addition, parents might structure their daughters' free time more closely than their sons' time, either to protect them or to make sure they have time for household chores. The result is that many girls have fewer chances for informal, after-school computer use.

And finally, some parents and educators accept the stereotypical notion that computers are more suitable for boys than for girls and convey that message to children.

## CLOSING THE GENDER GAP

The key to closing the gender gap in computer use is recognizing it exists—and that recognition must begin at the top in your school system. Teachers must operate within guidelines established by school boards and superintendents. Given the widespread community support for computer education, school board members are relatively free to set bold policy that will ensure equitable computer access and use in schools throughout their school systems. In doing so, you enable personnel already concerned about the computer gender gap to take effective action—and you provide a structure for those who have not yet discovered the problem to learn about it and contribute to its resolution.

Here are some suggestions for policy action your school board can take to address problems involving computer use and equity:

*Increase optional access*. A supervised computer laboratory should be available to students whenever possible during the school day and certainly after school, just as the school library is. Both are resources for class assignments and enrichment opportunities.

*Set a policy on software*. If you believe (as I do) that violent software is not healthy for children's social and emotional development (that goes for boys as well as girls), your policy should reflect that belief. You might want to stipulate that school funds cannot be used to purchase violent computer games and that school computers cannot be used to play them. Beyond that, it is helpful to stock your computer lab with word processing graphics, data-base, and spreadsheet programs that will be useful to both girls and boys in and out of the classroom.

*Provide training in computer use*. The sooner you consider computers as ordinary as textbooks—and use them as widely—the more equitable computer use will be in your schools. Teachers need training not only in how to operate computers, but also in how to use them in everyday teaching.

*Require students to take certain computer courses*. Optional computer courses appeal most to students who already like to use computers, and that means more boys than girls sign up. When you make introductory computer courses required fare—including thorough, hands-on training in all kinds of computer use—you guarantee that girls get the solid foundation they need to stay interested in computers.

*Provide sex equity training*. If staff members have not had in-service training in sex equity lately, now is a good time to schedule a session or two on computer equity.

*Assign women to your computer staff*. When it comes to computing, girls have few female role models: More fathers than mothers use computers; the news media are more likely to show men at computers than women; and school computer authorities most often are male. To redress this imbalance, encourage female applicants to apply when there's an opening for a computer teacher or coordinator in your schools.

*Counteract sex stereotyping*. To educate parents on the issue, discuss computer equity at a parent-teacher meeting. Make sure your teachers understand the need for special encouragement for girls to use computers, and encourage female teachers to use computers extensively themselves. If your schools offer a course on computers in society (or the equivalent), include an examination of sex stereotyping in the computer world.

One word of warning: Many schools have computers, but few have good computer programs. Because most teachers (and therefore most students) have little notion of what computers are good for, the machines are not used as fully as they might be. And although dozens of interesting and worthwhile activities designed to increase girls' computer use are available, teachers and principals seem unable to resist the understandable temptation to create a much-needed *educational computer* program but not an equally needed *computer equity* program. In other words, school people choose strategies designed to get the computer widely used by teachers and students in general, on the trickle-down theory that infusion alone will close the computer gender gap.

Computer pervasiveness is an important—maybe even an essential—part of getting girls involved with the machines, but it is not enough. The proof: Many schools with excellent computer education programs still have a computer gender gap. Instituting a high-quality computer education program increases the overall level of computer use, but in the end, the gap remains.

Achieving computer equity requires concentration on increasing computer use by girls in particular, as well as by students in general. To be sure, making available word processing, graphics, and other computer applications with special appeal to girls inevitably will improve computer education for boys as well; in fact, I've never seen any kind of sex equity program in a school that has not improved the educational environment for boys as well as for girls. In other words, if you insist on increasing girls' computer use, chances are *all* students will benefit. If you don't insist on computer equity, you'll just perpetuate an unnecessary gap.

One place to look for help in closing that gap is the Computer Equity Training Project. This project is funded by a grant from the Women's Educational Equity Act Program, U.S. Department of Education, to research the computer gender gap at the middle school level and develop remedies for it. Our project focuses on *optional* computer use—choosing to use the computer for class assignments or during free periods and before or after school—because that is where the gap is most visible. (It's not terribly difficult to achieve sex balance in computer use in a required course.)

Research shows that the more students use computers, the more likely they are to continue with computer study. That means girls who avoid computers now might continue to do so later—to their eventual regret. As adults, nine out of ten of them will work outside their homes. And according to the U.S. Department of Labor, from 50 to 75 percent of the jobs available in the next generation will involve computers in some way—from simple button pushing to sophisticated program design. Computer careers already yield more dollars per hour than do traditionally female occupations requiring the same amount of education, and the pattern is expected to continue. There's no question: Ignorance of computers will be a serious handicap in the job market in the years to come.

To help ensure that girls don't foreclose their career options, our project conducted pilot tests of computer equity strategies at schools in Wisconsin, Oregon, and New Jersey last year.* We've put the lessons we learned in those schools into a forthcoming book, *The Neuter Computer: Why and How to Encourage Computer Equity for Girls*. Currently, we are field-testing the book in new computer equity programs in schools in Vermont, Nebraska, and California,* and we expect to publish it this fall.

*The Neuter Computer* will contain dozens of computer equity strategies that can be put into effect by individual teachers, at the building level, and districtwide. In the meantime, though, your leadership in policymaking is essential: You must provide the resources and create the climate in which computer equity is recognized for the important educational issue it is.

*The schools that participated in last year's pilot: Franklin Junior High School in Whitewater, Wis.; Waldport Junior High School in Waldport, Ore.; and Mt. Hebron Middle School in Upper Montclair, N.J. The schools participating in current field tests: Camel's Hump Middle School in Richmond, Vt.; Gering Junior High School in Gering, Neb.; and Nobel Junior High School in Los Angeles. Lamar at Trenton Middle School in McAllen, Texas, is the control site.

# *Programming for Boys, Word Processing for Girls*

**by Art Luehrmann**

*Arthur Luehrmann is founding partner of the firm Computer Literacy in Berkeley, California.*

Prestigious national commissions, state agencies, educational leaders, and computer experts say again and again that being able to tell a computer what to do is a basic skill that *all* students should acquire. Yet, even in a school district with a strong computer education program, a visit to the computer classroom will show how far away this goal is.

Drop in and you'll probably see more boys than girls, and very few minority students. Ask the students there a few questions and you'll find above-average affluence, more likelihood of having a computer at home, better grades in academic subjects and so on. All measures of advantage, power, and prestige show up in the computer classroom.

The causes of this imbalance lie in the society as a whole. Three out of four computer campers are boys, almost exclusively white. Four out of five subscribers to popular computer magazines are men. Among entering freshmen at University of California at Berkeley, twice as many men as women have a computer at home or have written a computer program.

In this social context, why would anyone be surprised at the widely reported fact that twice as many boys as girls enroll in elective computer literacy classes or that certain minorities are underrepresented?

## A MISGUIDED SOLUTION

Can a change of school policy remedy this inequity? Yes, without a doubt. However, certain proposed changes only give the appearance of remedy. Consider this seductive line of reasoning: Current computer literacy courses emphasize learning to write programs. Girls and minority students don't like programming, so they don't elect today's courses. If course content changed, things would be different; therefore, the argument goes, the emphasis should be shifted away from programming and toward useful applications like word processing.

Although deeply defective, the argument does have surface appeal. Students would learn immediately applicable skills: writing papers, organizing information, drawing graphs, etc. They wouldn't have to work as hard at learning programming, which is fine since few will follow careers as programmers. Girls and minority students who shun today's computer classes would be less turned off by the new emphasis.

---

From *Electronic Learning*, February 1985. Reprinted with permission from Scholastic, Inc.

But apply the same argument to eighth-grade math. Girls and minority students (and quite a few boys) don't seem terribly drawn to algebra. Few students will follow careers as mathematicians, much less algebraists. Algebra skills are not immediately applicable. Shouldn't we rather teach a different sort of math course—one that shows how to use arithmetic to help with adding a grocery bill, balancing a checkbook, and scoring a track meet?

## WHY LEARN THINGS?

Yet schools insist that *everybody* try to learn algebra rather than take a dead-end class in math applications. Why? Not because the paper is full of want ads for algebraists. Not because average adults sit around solving algebra problems all the time. Rather, schools insist on algebra because of its *intellectual significance* and because it is a *prerequisite* for more work in math and related subjects.

Programming skills should be viewed in the same light. Using an application program written by someone else may be easier than learning to write programs of one's own, but it would be foolish to claim that word processing skills, for example, are on the same intellectual level as programming skills. The first gives the student only minimal control over the computer and few basic ideas about it. Programming skills give complete control and deep ideas about computers.

Just as any student who intends to go on in math must learn algebra, so any student who wishes to go beyond the first course in computing must learn to solve problems by writing programs. *Knowing how to operate application programs is not a prerequisite to any course in school or college. Programming is a prerequisite to all computer courses after the first.*

What will happen, then, if misguided school planners, eager to attract women and minorities, remove programming instruction from the introductory computer class? The answer is obvious: Girls and minority students will learn word processing and then drop out of computing because they lack essential skills for going on. The more savvy students, mostly white and male, will opt for the programming class and be ready for a different future. Inequity will be reinforced.

## A SIMPLE SOLUTION

There is a simple solution. Do what schools now do about math equity, language equity, and science equity: Define a curriculum that prepares students to go on in that field; then require all students to take it.

In the case of the required computer class, the content backbone is the skill to express ideas in a programming language, and to solve problems. This solid content opens doors that word processing skills do not even crack.

A conventional solution like this won't eliminate all inequity, but it will deal more directly and honestly with the problem than any attempt to remove the "hard" or "unattractive" parts of computer literacy, an attempt that sells short the very people one claims to help.

# *The Information Age and the Schools*

**by Henry S. Kepner, Jr.**

*Henry S. Kepner, Jr., is Professor of Curriculum and Instruction, responsible for computer education and mathematics education at the University of Wisconsin-Milwaukee.*

The computer presents an opportunity for schools to collect, organize, and interpret data in ways and magnitudes seldom previously available to the educational system. This expanded capability now is available for administrators, teachers, and students alike. The challenge for education is to find and implement ways to turn large amounts of data into meaningful and useful information for so wide a variety of users with many needs.

In the schools, there are a multitude of instances in which decisions are made on some, but not sufficient, information. Teachers make numerous instructional decisions concerning students during every lesson. In what ways can teachers receive assistance in making such decisions? Students continually are expected to learn new ideas and skills. Beyond the direct instruction part of the curriculum, how can students learn to find, organize, and use the information available for their learning and individual needs? Computer technology is available to assist in these tasks. How can it best be used? Administrators are continually responsible for making decisions that affect the entire school, as well as the community. What training is necessary to help them make decisions with the best collection of data possible?

In addition, how can we prevent people from misusing computer data? The issues relating to the misuse of data come from several directions. First, there is the frequently reported use of or tampering with data that does not "belong" to the person viewing that material. Second, there is the use of data by persons who do not have the background to interpret it in a meaningful way. This problem can easily lead to decision making that is incorrect. Such decisions can be harmful to individual students, or to the entire community. Third, there is the issue of deciding who will have access to the collected data. Here, the balancing of individual privacy with the need for assigned decision makers to have access to the data for the good of the district is of great concern in dealing with students. An additional dilemma occurs when one segment of the district has access to information that is denied to a competing segment of the population. For example, does a school board incumbent get critical information on the school and its performance that is denied an outside candidate for the board position?

## THE TEACHER

For the classroom teacher, computer-assisted instruction promises additional information on and monitoring of students as they move through the curriculum. First, the computer can present the teacher's or courseware developer's sequence of instructional lessons as selected in advance. With adequate computer power and effective computer-based lessons, the teacher has the opportunity to provide a different sequence of instruction for each student. Despite this historical goal, teachers seldom have been able to provide such individual attention to students in the classroom setting.

Second, the classroom teacher can be presented with a large array of data that may be useful in making instructional decisions at several levels of complexity. Existing technology permits the recording of student responses during computer-assisted instruction or computer testing. Results can be reported and acted on instantly by either the teacher or the computer. In this respect, student errors can be addressed almost immediately, not one to two days later after grading a student's paper.

As our knowledge of student errors grows and computer technology improves, the opportunity to provide more instruction under computer control is possible. Instructional computing programs can be constructed to anticipate common student errors in skill areas of the curriculum. For example, a student may get subtraction exercises wrong because he/she always subtracts the "smaller number" from the "bigger number" in each column of the subtraction exercise. If the student makes that error, the computer can be programmed to notice it. The courseware can include lessons specifically for students who make that error; only students who make that error will get the special lessons.

Third, extensive student records can be compiled to show the extent of student performance on school content, areas of difficulty, and other data collected over the child's involvement in the school.

While the computer collects data on student performance, there are serious questions about the ability of teachers to use it effectively to improve instruction. One important consideration is the training of classroom teachers. Few practicing teachers have adequate background to allow them to assimilate and act on all the additional data the computer could generate on each student. When teachers first begin to work with computer-based materials, they are overwhelmed by "information overload." So much data is presented that the teacher becomes unable to make decisions. Two levels of action are required to help teachers use computer-based instruction effectively. First, the curriculum team, including content specialists, educational psychologists, and measurement experts must learn what data is most valuable so that they can present key information to the teacher. Also, they must provide suggestions for appropriate decision making based on the information presented. Second, teacher training sessions must be developed to help teachers work in a new environment where instructional decisions are based on computer printouts as well as on classroom observations.

As computer-based curriculum materials are entering the educational system, teachers must be trained to use them appropriately. When a teacher turns the student over to a computer for practice or instruction, the computer presents the student with content and sequence that have been developed by someone outside of the immediate setting. Except for its programmed ability to recognize and respond to certain types of student errors, the computer-based instruction is not likely to be flexible in response to other student difficulties. A human teacher is a critical component in learning situations. The teacher has a responsibility to make certain that the student goes to the computer with adequate prerequisite skills, and to monitor performance regularly so that the student isn't overwhelmed by computer-generated tasks.

One of the most common misuses of computers in the classroom today is individual drill before the student is ready for it. The result can be no learning, reinforcement of an incorrect or inappropriate technique, or intense student frustration in a computer-controlled practice setting. Too frequently, a teacher sends a student to a computer drill on the basic addition facts before he/she has sophisticated strategies for generating answers to drill questions. If still counting on his/her fingers, the student will likely increase his/her proficiency and speed at finger counting to get sums, rather than develop more mature strategies for getting sums. This misuse of computer-controlled instruction can stunt developmental growth in a subject.

Since it is likely that the teacher did not develop the software, the teacher must be aware of its limitations for students who use it. Many software packages generate exercises for the student until he/she completes the task. If a student gets most of them wrong, the computer may continue to present such tasks to him. With this type of software, the teacher must be alert to get the student off the computer until further instruction can occur. Otherwise, the student faces the same situation faced in doing homework with inadequate knowledge—the student practices numerous exercises with an incorrect procedure.

## THE STUDENT

Students are becoming familiar with the computer in the schools. According to the most recent data, there are over one million computers, mostly microcomputers, in elementary and secondary schools in the United States. Up to the present time, most student contact has been limited to drill and practice software that did little but ask questions and reinforce responses. Now there is the opportunity for students to use the computer to retrieve, and even create, information through the use of data base, spreadsheet or word processor software.

In preparing to gather necessary information, students should have experience in using information retrieval software along with other library skills currently practiced in the school program. The ability to enter and use a system like ERIC, The Source, or CompuServe, will be helpful in locating sources of information on a given topic. While far from comprehensive in many areas, these retrieval systems identify extensive sources of information on topics selected by the construction of a logical statement using key words from the system vocabulary. For example, students must learn that the statement, "American OR soccer OR heroes" will locate all sources that are keyed for any of the three terms, while the statement "American AND soccer AND heroes" will isolate sources that are keyed to contain all three references.

The ability to use an information retrieval system is extremely valuable to students. Use of such a tool often gives the student access, or at least knowledge of sources of information that are not available in the school, or even in the town library. In using such a system to generate a list of appropriate sources on a given topic, the student has gained awareness of information that is available on that topic. Through electronic communications, it is possible to retrieve abstracts, or even copies, of the materials that appear promising to the student researcher. For example, one of the early data base systems, The Source, projected that all of the material in the Library of Congress would be stored on its computer system by the turn of the century. With that much data in a system, the user of that system has access to a tremendous amount of information instantly at any computer terminal. Skill at searching such a huge collection of information for the needed works will be a critical research skill for an educated person.

While most individuals will use data bases constructed by others, students should learn how to construct an organized set of data for their own use. For example, one student may create an organized record of the baseball player cards collected. This data base could include the name, years played, team, and positions played for each player. Then subsets of player cards could be identified by any one or a combination of the categories chosen. Thus, the student could obtain a list of cards for players who played outfield for the Dodgers in 1980. If additional information on the teams was entered—such as league, division, and location—the student could retrieve the list of player cards for all outfielders who played for teams in the Western Divison of the National League in 1980.

Another student may set up a data base that contains data on all the customers on a paper route. Such a data base can be constantly updated to reflect customer address, telephone number and payments; the dates for starting or stopping of service; and specific customer demands. Such a data base can be used to keep accurate records and to provide a list of customers for a substitute delivery person. The opportunity to create data bases gives students neeeded experience in selecting data that will be valuable in carrying out a task. The current school curriculum provides too little opportunity for students to make such decisions.

While the experiences of using and creating data bases are important components to accessing information in the computer age, students must also learn the limits of any data base they use. In using existing bases, one should know what sources of information are included and what sources are not included. For example, an ERIC search includes articles from certain periodicals. Key information in another periodical will not be shown in the original search.

In using a word processor, the user creates a document that can be examined and changed at will. Each time the user returns to the document, it can be altered and stored for future reference. Students should learn to use this electronic tool in writing when they will be doing enough writing to warrant its use. This computer tool allows ease of revision as well as the opportunity to use computer programs to check spelling.

Use of computer technology in the above tasks gives students a powerful tool. In addition to using it appropriately, they must also consider misuses of this technology. Like learning to use a firearm or to drive a car, the individual should learn acceptable behaviors with such an instrument, along with learning the skills required in its use. Today, the schools are paying little attention to this element of computer literacy. Many of the abuses of computer information technology are represented by the things that happen in early computer experiences. At these occurrences, students should explore acceptable computer behavior.

During early computer work, students often play pranks on others, such as turning off the power while someone is on the computer, or placing swear words in the middle of another student's program or document which is stored on a computer disk. Such activities can become appropriate learning situations if these students are asked to consider the consequences of their acts from the vantage points of the several individuals involved. As with other forms of accepted behavior, students quickly learn what things are not fun to the recipient of the "joke."

When theft or tampering is done to a valued word-processed document or data base of an individual, others can experience and empathize with the loss and feelings of that individual. Through the social science technique of "moral dilemmas" discussion, small groups and classes can help build student abilities to reason about ethical concerns in computer use. The extension of personal experiences to dilemmas about breaking into medical or defense data banks is a necessary follow-up for students today. From such situations, students can see the need to protect their own information and programs from unwanted intrusions. Just as is the lock on our front door, computer security is a necessary tool for all of us.

A practical example of dealing with computer ethics occurs in every school where the students have gained minimal computer skills. Consider the situation where a paper is due in all the junior English classes. Mary has completed her paper for Mr. Jones on the word processor. Bill hasn't started his paper for Mrs. Tilden. On the morning the assignment is due, Bill approaches Mary about making a copy of her paper for him to turn in. Both students are sure that the two different teachers will not catch the duplicate paper. What should Mary do? This dilemma requires students to evaluate their reason for being in school. Students, teachers, and parents are all involved in this dilemma. What are the ethical factors to consider?

A second volatile issue in our capitalistic society is the illegal copying of copyrighted software. For students and too many teachers, this is often seen as an appropriate thing to do. After all, if you own a good program, such as a game or useful program, I can benefit by making an electronic copy of your program. After making the copy, you get your original back. In contrast to other materials ownership, it appears that there is no harm done to either of us.

These are only a sample of the misuses that students should consider as they gain technical knowledge of computer operation. As in any area of technological advance, students should understand both uses and misuses of such technology. In addition, they should learn of society's attempt to monitor or regulate abuses.

## SUMMARY

Computers in the schools provide students, teachers, and administrators with a new technology for collecting data and turning it into useful information. However, before we can expect this to happen, the user must obtain some skills in using the computer and must also gain some experience in using the computer as a tool in the decision-making process. As well as learning the positive uses of information processing on the computer, individuals must be aware of the appropriate use of computer technology in our democratic society.

# *Suggested Readings for Computer Equity and Funding*

**by Henry S. Kepner, Jr.**


1. Brady, Holly, and Slesnick, Twila. "Girls Don't Like Fluffware Either." *Classroom Computer Learning* 5, no. 8 (April–May 1985): 22–27.

   A report showing that most software doesn't have much appeal for girls, including the software written specifically for them. Includes a summary of research on how girls lose interest in computer learning.

2. Burnham, David. *The Rise of the Computer State*. New York: Vintage Books, 1984.

   A frightening, yet thoughtful, presentation on the potential of computers to destroy individual privacy, this book raises the reader's awareness about the need to set safeguards on information access and use.

3. "Computer Equity Theme Issue." *The Computing Teacher* 11, no. 8 (April 1984).

   This special issue of *The Computing Teacher* has more than twenty articles addressing the computer equity issue from both philosophical and practical views. Major emphasis is given to female, minority, and handicapped access to computers both during the school day, and through community and off-hours approaches. The ideas and reports on successful programs are a must for a district addressing equity in computing.

4. Eaton, Marian S., et al. "Out-of-School Computer Access: An Equity Issue." *The Computing Teacher* 12, no. 9 (June 1985): 20–21.

   A brief, but important consideration of the opportunities and choices girls and boys make about computers outside the classroom. The authors raise key issues on school intervention possibilities.

5. Inose, Hiroshi, and Pierce, John. *Information Technology and Civilization*. New York: W. H. Freeman & Co., 1984.

   This perceptive report on the anticipated impact of information technology on society was prepared originally for a Club of Rome annual meeting. Giving equal attention to potentialities and problems, it emphasizes how information technology may affect learning, the arts, government, and individuals.

6. Kepner, Henry S., Jr., ed. *Computers in the Classroom*. 2d ed. Washington, D.C.: National Education Association, 1986.

   Examining the key issues in the use of computers in instruction, this book focuses on their varied uses across the disciplines. The computer is presented only as a tool for education, not as a solution to all educational problems.

7. Logsdon, Tom. *Computers and Social Controversy*. Rockville, Md.: Computer Science Press, 1980.

   This book offers in-depth sections on the issues of electronic privacy intrusion, computer fraud, electronic fund transfer systems, automation, machines that teach, artificial intelligence, and the geopolitics of computers.

8. Nora, Simon, and Minc, Alain. *The Computerization of Society*. Cambridge: The MIT Press, 1981.

Written as a report to the president of France, this book presents a vision of how a new technology can reshape society and discusses why the political system must respond to the new economic and social life that result.

9. Norman, Adrian. *Computer Security*. New York: Chapman and Hall, 1985.

In a discussion of the new issues of computer misuse, computer crime, and computer vulnerability, the author argues that problems are larger than technical security; they include human failures. The author recommends positive ways to manage computer risks.

10. Office of Technology Assessment. *Information Technology and Its Impact on American Education*. Washington, D.C.: U.S. Government Printing Office, 1982.

This wide-ranging report emphasizes the stresses placed on social institutions, such as public schools and libraries, which traditionally have borne the major responsibility for providing public education and information services. Changes in education and access to information are considered, and projections about federal involvement in schools and libraries are presented.

11. Rothman, Stanley, and Mosmann, Charles. *Computer Uses and Issues*. Chicago: Science Research Associates, 1985.

A good introduction to computers, this book emphasizes computers in educational settings, with sections on resulting technical and social issues.

12. Schug, Mark, and Kepner, Henry S., Jr. "Helping Students Deal with Computer Issues in Social Studies." *Georgia Social Science Journal* 16 (Winter 1985): 5–15.

This article outlines the major components of computer literacy for all students, giving special attention to helping students in social studies programs understand the individual and social questions raised by the growth of computer use.

13. "Women in Technology." Special section in *Technology Review* (November–December 1984): 29–50, ff.

A set of articles examining the changes and barriers facing women entering computer technology fields. These articles are written for the scientific community, but are important sources for school career settings. Articles include: Lilli S. Hornig, "Women in Science and Engineering: Why So Few?"; H. Patricia Hynes, "Women Working: A Field Report"; Sharon Traweek, "High-Energy Physics: A Male Preserve"; Evelyn Fox Keller, "Women and Basic Research: Respecting the Unexpected"; and Sherry Turkle, "Women and Computer Programming: A Different Approach."

14. Yin, Robert K., and White, J. Lynne. *Microcomputer Implementation in Schools*. COSMOS Corporation, 1730 K Street, N.W., Suite 1302, Washington, D.C. 1984.

"A report which describes and analyzes the experiences of twelve school districts in using microcomputers in their schools and district offices. The report focuses on the *organizational* aspects of the implementation process." This statement from the report identifies the value of this study to those responsible for bringing computers into schools or making some sense out of the stream of hardware and software already flowing into the district.

# *Computer Technology Terms*

**ADMINISTRATIVE SOFTWARE.** Applications software designed to solve administrative problem(s).

**APPLICATIONS SOFTWARE.** A program written to serve a function or solve a problem not related to the operation of the computer system.

**ARITHMETIC/LOGIC UNIT.** The unit of a computer that performs the arithmetic and logical operations.

**AUTHORING SOFTWARE.** Computer programs that enable a courseware developer (author) to generate computer-assisted instruction and/or computer-managed instruction.

**BILINGUAL EDUCATION.** Intended for persons whose primary language is not English. It provides instruction in academic subjects in the student's native language until the student has achieved sufficient mastery of English to use it for the study of the curriculum.

**BRANCHING.** A computer operation in which a selection is made between two or more possible courses of action depending upon user input.

**BREAK POINTS.** Stopping points designed into the courseware to allow for termination of a session before the actual conclusion of the unit of study.

**CATHODE RAY TUBE (CRT).** An output device that gives a visual display of text and graphics from a computer (similar to a television screen).

**CENTRAL PROCESSING UNIT (CPU).** A control unit of a computer that directs information in and out of the different parts of the computer.

**CODE.** The symbolic text of a program. This is the form in which programs are written and read by programmers.

**COMPUTER.** A device that can input, store, manipulate, and output data. A computer has five (5) main parts: Input Device(s), Memory, Arithmetic/Logic Unit, Central Processing Unit (CPU), and Output Device(s).

**COMPUTER-ASSISTED INSTRUCTION (CAI).** A computer software application in which a computer is used to conduct instruction utilizing such techniques as text screens, graphics screens, etc.

**COMPUTER INTERACTIVE VIDEO (CIV).** An integrated system using the capabilities of the computer and audiovisual media for instruction. User input enables the computer program to select both the appropriate sequences and the appropriate computer responses.

**COMPUTER-MANAGED INSTRUCTION (CMI).** A computer software application in which a computer is used to sequence, branch, test, prescribe, and track progress and report on user input, but not to conduct instruction.

**COURSEWARE.** Educational applications software used for teaching and learning.

**CURSOR.** The graphic notation on the screen identifying the user's point of entry for any input into the computer.

**DATA.** A collection of factual information for processing.

**DATA BASE.** A collection of information (data), large or small, about any particular subject or group of subjects.

**DELETE/BACK SPACE.** A key on the computer keyboard that is used to erase commands and correct typing mistakes before RETURN is hit to enter the commands into the computer.

**DIGITAL SCREEN.** Monitor displaying text generated by a computer program.

**DISKETTE.** A magnetically coated, record-shaped object used to store data. (Also called a "floppy disk.")

**DOCUMENTATION.** A collection of written or printed materials that aid in the understanding of a computer system or program.

**DRILL AND PRACTICE.** Computer programs to reinforce learning through repeated examples and questions related to a particular subject being taught.

**DUBBING.** Reproduction of visual or audio images from one source or medium to another.

**ENGLISH AS A SECOND LANGUAGE.** Intended for students whose primary language is other than English. For them, it provides instruction to achieve proficiency in English speaking, reading, and writing.

**EXTERNAL SOFTWARE.** Software, other than the operating system and the courseware, required to use the courseware on a computer system.

**FEEDBACK.** The computer's response to the particular input of the user.

**GRAPHICS.** Output displayed in representational or pictorial form, such as histograms, maps, or graphs.

**HARD COPY.** A printed copy of machine output in a visually readable form, such as printed reports, listings, documents, and summaries.

**HARDWARE.** The physical parts of a computer (mechanical, magnetic, electrical, and electronic devices).

**HELP FUNCTION.** The capability within the computer program for the user to call up and receive assistance in using the program.

**INPUT.** The data that go into the computer to be processed.

**INPUT DEVICE.** A mechanical device used to transmit the input into the computer.

**INTERACTIVE CAPABILITY.** A computer system or program designed to allow an interchange (dialogue) between the user at a keyboard (or other input device) and the computer during the execution of a program.

**INTERACTIVITY.** The capability of the computer program to proceed along different sequences of screens or prompts (i.e., to branch), depending on the input of the user. In other words, the program proceeds differently given different user inputs.

**INTERFACE.** The electronic elements (hardware and/or software) which either connect the computer to peripheral devices or connect different elements of the computer to each other.

**INTEGRATED SYSTEM.** Two or more electronic components forming a working computer application in which all the components are essential for operation, each fulfilling a different function.

**LIGHT PEN.** A hand-held, light-sensing device that is detected by the CRT when pointed toward a portion of the screen.

**LOCKOUT CODES.** A procedure coded in a program to verify that a user is permitted to access software.

**MACHINE READABLE.** Data input into a computer without keystrokes, such as from disk, magnetic tape, or documents usable for optical character recognition (OCR).

**MAGNETIC MEDIUM.** An electronically treated material (usually plastic) which can store electrical signals for transmission to electronic devices (parts of a computer) under the stimulus of an electrical current.

**MENU.** A list of the features and/or segments of a program that is displayed on the screen and from which the user can select the next operation option.

**MICROCOMPUTER.** A computer designed primarily for use by one person at a time and which contains the five parts of a computer. See COMPUTER.

**MONITOR**. See CATHODE RAY TUBE.

**MOUSE.** A special device that allows the user to move a cursor on the computer screen in any direction—up or down, diagonally, left or right, or in a circle. When the cursor is properly positioned on the screen, the user can then designate his/her selection.

**OPERATING SYSTEM.** Software that controls the execution of computer programs and may provide scheduling, input/output control, data management, and related services.

**OPTICAL CHARACTER RECOGNITION.** The process of reading characters or other symbols through the use of light-sensitive devices.

**OUTPUT.** Data that have been processed in a computer and are transferred from the CPU to an external device (e.g., printer, screen).

**PERIPHERAL.** Any piece of equipment, distinct from the computer itself, that allows the computer either to receive input from or deliver output to another device (e.g., printer, monitor, keyboard).

**PRINTOUT.** Information or output from the computer printed on paper.

**PRODUCTION VALUES.** Technical qualities and standards for an audio or visual product, such as the believability of the sets, acting, and scripts in a video production or the accuracy of the sound reproduction on a tape or sound tract.

**PROGRAM.** A set of coded instructions written in sequence that tell the computer what to do.

**PROGRAMMING CODE.** See CODE.

**RANDOM ORDER.** Questions and problems presented by the courseware appearing in a different (random) sequence during each session using the courseware.

**RECORD KEEPING.** The computer's capability of storing the user's responses to questions, scoring them, and having them available for retrieval.

**REPORT GENERATION.** The computer's capability of producing reports based on the records (i.e., student performance) that it has stored.

**RETURN.** A key on the computer keyboard that completes a user entry and transmits it to the computer for processing.

**SCREEN DISPLAY.** Use of a CRT for display of output from the computer, including instructional text, questions, and responses.

**SIMULATION (CAI).** A type of computer-assisted instruction that imitates a real operation or scenario of some type, such as the operation of an aircraft control panel.

**SOFTWARE.** A (set of) program(s) written in a computer language (e.g., Basic, COBOL) which enables a computer to receive and to process data.

**SOURCE LISTING.** A print copy of the code. See CODE.

**SPECIAL DEVICES.** Special-purpose peripheral equipment. See PERIPHERAL.

**SPECIAL EFFECTS.** Sounds or visual additions to the primary material presented, whether on the computer program or on the visual image. These can be computer-generated still or moving graphic displays, overlays, or various other audio or visual additions to attract attention to or emphasize the primary material.

**STORAGE CAPACITY.** The amount of data and code that can be stored in the computer system, usually expressed in kilobytes (k) or thousands of bytes.

**TEACHER'S MANUAL.** Documentation provided to the teacher containing information concerning the operation of the software (how to run the program) and its instructional design and characteristics.

**TECHNICAL MANUAL.** Documentation provided to the user that describes the functions of the software and indicates how to use the software.

**TERMINAL.** A device, usually equipped with a keyboard and some kind of output device, capable of sending and receiving information over a communication channel.

**TEST DATA.** Data organized to aid in the testing of the software, allowing for all features to be exercised.

**TOUCH SCREEN.** A CRT screen equipped with a position sensor so that finger contact causes the coordinates of the point touched to be transmitted to a computer.

**TRACKING.** The computer's capability to store the input and sequence of the user through the computer program.

**TUTORIAL.** A type of computer-assisted instruction (CAI) that presents a question, judges the student's response, and tutors the student when an incorrect response is received. In tutorial CAI, an attempt to diagnose the source of the student's problem is frequently made; the tutoring is thereby interactive.

**USER.** A person or organization that utilizes a computer system.

**VIDEODISC (LASER).** Audiovisual material prerecorded on a durable plastic disc. A single disc can store one hour of continuous play video images (108,000 frames) and up to two sound tracks. A videodisc player allows quick random access to any one of the disc's 54,000 frames per side or to a series of frames. It will search forward or reverse and play at standard speed, in slow motion, or frame by frame. Videodisc usually refers to storage of analog signals. The same technology can be used to store digital signals and is usually called CD ROM.

**VOICE INPUT.** Voice communication with the computer system. Voice transmission of data to be processed.

**VOICE OUTPUT.** Audio transmission of output from the computer system.

# *The NEA Educational Computer Service*

The National Education Association has been active in educational technology matters since the 1960s, principally by issuing policy recommendations, legislative reports, and research findings. The "computer revolution" of the 1980s, however, has presented our teachers with a whole new set of needs. In 1986, the installed base of computers in American schools is approaching two million units, nearly ten times the number just four years ago. Today virtually every teacher, every school building, and every school district in the United States has at least some contact with computer-based education.

To address teachers' needs, the NEA determined that, along with other actions, it would advocate the development and distribution of "schoolworthy" software. It focused on software because this is the "intelligence" of a computer application. Software is to a computer what film is to a movie projector; it is the substance of the end product. The Association's decision led to the establishment in 1983 of the NEA Educational Computer Service, a special-focus group which has pursued an aggressive campaign to establish and promote high-quality standards for schoolworthy software.

In May 1986, NEA announced a new program of the Service, which is intended to focus particularly on the quality of courseware and to recognize and congratulate the publishers of "The Best" such products in one or more categories each year. These products will be chosen through a national competition with the participation of the entire NEA membership.

The overriding purpose of the NEA Educational Computer Service is to make it easy for the teachers and students of America to participate in the computer revolution. The mission is, first of all, a service to our members and their students. Ultimately it constitutes a public service. We realize that this is a complex and ambitious undertaking, but with the assistance of the 1.8 million teachers of the NEA, as well as the authors, publishers, and users of educational software, we can make a difference.

For more information on the NEA Educational Computer Service, write to

NEA Educational Computer Service
Instruction and Professional Development
NEA Center
1201 16th Street, NW
Washington, DC 20036

nea

Stock No. 1535-5